Start Your Own Successful Small Business

From Idea to Launch

How to Write an Effective Business Plan Step By Step

I0477505

By

Thomas Winfield

Cover & Book Design by Emily Jacobs

Inside This Book

INTRODUCTION

Starting a business isn't an easy task, and that is putting it lightly. As an economically-successful business owner, I'm speaking from my personal experiences throughout that path. I didn't have a guide or someone to teach me; I just learned as I went along, trying this and that, using what worked and discarding what did not.

For the most part, instructional videos are helpful, and reading articles on the subject will always give you a better idea of where to go and what to do. But in the end, it was only through my own conviction and hard work that

I was able to get through those first few steps toward pushing for my first business, and through even more patience that I managed to keep it afloat until it to become fruitful enough so I could leave my office job.

A factor you will have to understand about business-building is that there is no such thing as failure. The simple act of attempting something you have a good feeling about is something not many people even bother to do, regardless of whether it reaches a successful outcome.

If your first few tries at creating your own business do not work the way you believed they would make it a point to understand what should be improved, brush yourself off, and give it another go until you find a formula that works for you. It is all about keeping an open mind to the possibilities and to what you are inherently talented at.

With that being said, I want to help others not make the same mistakes I did, which is exactly why I'm writing this guide for you. This way you are able to cut several unnecessary corners and get to the actual concrete focus of what you are doing.

I started my own business because of several reasons, most of which involved financial freedom and wanting more time with my family by getting the opportunity to handle my own schedule. I'm going to show you how you can start your own business from idea to launch using what I have learned so far, and the experiences I've gathered in the last five years of looking after my own thriving small-scale business.

I'll tell you how it should be done so you can avoid making the common mistakes that plague new business owners as well as help you to see how you can juggle starting a new business while maintaining your normal job until you are able to focus on doing just that in the long run. So, let's get started.

WHY YOU SHOULD CONSIDER STARTING A BUSINESS

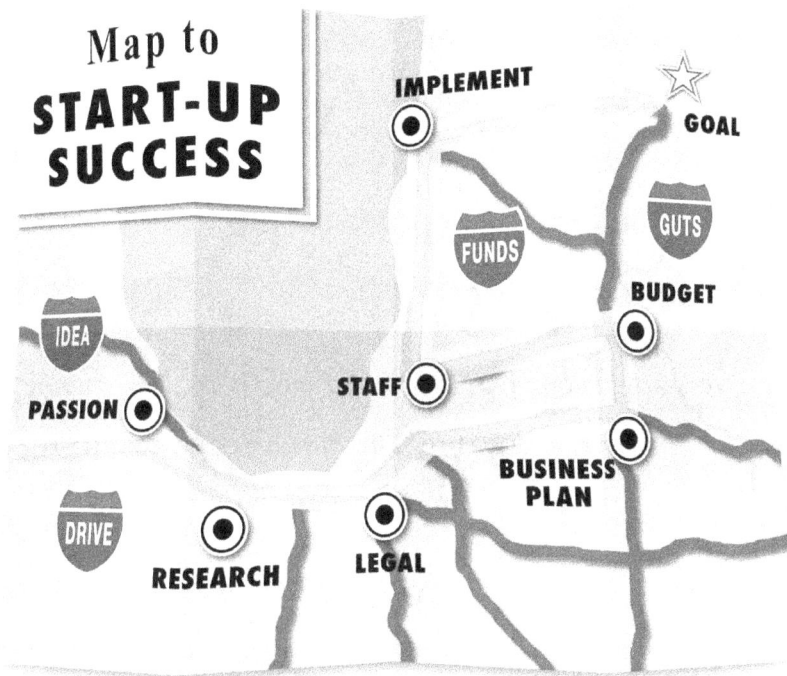

If you're reading this book, it is likely because you are thinking of starting a business. Perhaps you already know what you want to do and just want some guidance on how to get started.

My guess is that you aren't quite sure yet if you have what it takes or if you can even do it, which is why we are first going to assess that part before anything else. Let's take a look at the reasons why starting a business is a good idea, and how you are more than equipped to do so as long as you keep your head on your shoulders.

Let's start thinking about that business you want to start, and more importantly, why you want to start it in the first place. Having an idea of what you want to achieve is key in the direction you ought to take.

WORK ON WHAT YOU WANT

When you start your own business, you'll be able to work on projects you want or things that matter to you. You aren't stuck working on things that don't apply to you, but rather to the head of a company. In those cases, your boss ends up earning more money for your hard work, while you only get a small percentage in comparison to the big-scale offices in charge of your check.

With financial freedom, you would be able to quit that day job you hold on to because without it you might have to eat ramen for the next few months.

If you have a family, you know as much as I do that is not even an option, since other people are relying on you for housing and food. If you are the sort who loves working outside and has an innate talent in carving wood, starting your own furniture business would be able to sustain you and those around you.

If you love making jewelry with wire-wrapping techniques or colorful resin, you could begin selling your own jewelry on a platform you built. Soaps, candles, perfumes, food, metalworking, art, the sky's the limit so long as you have a goal, patience, and passion.

INCREASE IN INCOME

When you're an employee, there is a limit to how much money you can make, as we addressed. When you start your own business you will have greater control over how much you make and you can even use your business as a side job with passive income to help increase the amount of money you make each year, until you reach the level of success where you can quit your day job if you wish and focus solely on your business.

IMPROVED JOB SECURITY

While some people think that having a regular job is more secure than starting a new business venture, the fact is that starting your own business provides you with improved job security. Sometimes companies get bought out, or they choose to go in another direction.

For reasons A, B, or C, you could lose your job for the most random reasons possible, and a sense of panic and disappointment is bound to make your liver shrivel up until you find another employer.

In fact, you could dedicate a decade of your life to a company, only for it to consider you disposable the minute someone younger than you becomes the new CEO. For better or for worse, job security is not always an option.

On the other hand, owning your own business is a bit of a gamble, but since you will be your own employer, no one can possibly fire you, unless you were to enter a very strange dialogue with yourself.

Having a business allows you to make money outside of your regular job so you can diversify your income and gives you a backup option if you wish to keep working in your current gig.

Flexibility in Your Schedule

Perhaps the most difficult thing about a daily job is the fact that you probably already don't have time to do things like making a doctor's appointment, much less meet family in town for lunch or other fun activities.

Never mind the spontaneous trip if you need to ask for time off in advance that you may not always get. When you own your own business, you can set your own flexible schedule and possibly even take your job with you wherever you go so you can enjoy anything you want at any hour of your choosing, so long as it makes sense with your economic goals.

Whether you are on your own and wish to have some time to travel, study, explore, or visit friends and family, or whether you already have children or a spouse, and you wish to spend more hours of the day with them, having your own business could very well be the answer you've been looking for.

Better Tax Benefits

Starting a business comes with a few of monetary and tax benefits. You could write off things such as travel, food, and cell phone bills as part of your job depending on what you choose to center that around.

There is more of a sense of responsibility to upkeep your taxes as a small business, and never being dishonest about the numbers you are dealing with in your sales revenue.

To help keep everything organized, you will need a notebook or a computer file with all the logs of how many sales you made in a year, and how much of the money was reinvested back in the business for supplies or upgrades

IMPROVE YOUR QUALITY OF LIFE

Have you ever wanted to move somewhere else or have more freedom to improve your life? Whether it is to learn how to cook Mediterranean food, having a go at a new language, or simply sitting down with a good book on your lap and relaxing for an hour or two, you will attain this once your business starts creating a comfortable amount of revenue.

In a nutshell, when you own a business, you not only have geological freedom to go wherever you want and set your business wherever you want, but you can also give yourself more time to focus on your quality of life.

RETIRE EARLY

Perhaps one of the best reasons to start your own business is the opportunity to retire whenever you personally decide. You might even get a good routine in place where your self-assigned job will not feel like a chore or work, but rather like the building blocks of something you created–of something you hopefully enjoy doing so much on your spare time you thought of a stable way to make a profit out of it.

If you feel better about what you do, your retirement might just arrive before you know it, or even better, when you choose it.

SPEND MORE TIME WITH FAMILY

We've touched upon this subject here and there, but it deserves its own spot as a key reason to launch your own business. When I first had my own children, it made me anxious to think I was missing so much when I went to work every morning, and as they got older, I realized I was so tired from my job that I hardly had the energy to do much else other than eat dinner.

I hated the thought of not wanting to play games with my children because I simply did not have the energy. They did not deserve that.

It was around that time when my spouse suggested me having my own business, and that wish turned into a reality for me, just in time. It was not an immediate transition, and I would still be tired from handling two different business ventures, but I knew it would be worth it in the end.

Now that we know the reasons you currently have for starting your own business let's get into the basics of it. We need to start with your business idea. You may already have one, or you may simply know you want to start a business.

Whether it is time, financial freedom, travel, family, or a long-held dream, I'm going to help you get started with finding a business idea.

Startup Business Ideas

The first thing you need to do when coming up with a business idea is to look at yourself. Take a look at your own strengths and weaknesses, likes and dislikes. Next step is to show you how to evaluate yourself to help you look for these business ideas.

Make a List

Before you can evaluate yourself or start to think about business ideas, you want to start by creating two lists. This process can take about 30 minutes, so be prepared.

The first list will be focused on any business or entrepreneurship goals you want to achieve. You don't need to make this list so extensive that you write down all the skills needed to have a successful business.

Instead, you are looking for a general overview. Once you have the list finished, go back and highlight the skills that you already possess and place a star beside the ones you think you need to develop. Set this list aside and move on to the next one.

For the second list, you'll want to take an honest look at yourself without being neither too harsh with yourself nor too overconfident. You'll want to have two columns, one for strengths and one for weaknesses.

Based on your personality, one of these two columns will be easy to fill out if you are as objective as possible. Remember not to overthink any flaws and don't overestimate your strengths. Simply write things down and move on to the next item.

Again the final list doesn't have to be extensive, since having only about 10 items or less in each column is more than enough. This list will help to give you some general ideas about yourself, which you'll refine later with input from other trusted sources who know you well.

If you're having a hard time coming up with something for the list, consider asking yourself the following questions:

- ☐ What are you good at?

- ☐ What compliments have you received from others?

- ☐ What have you had to ask for help with on more than one occasion?

- ☐ What tasks and/or projects tend to drain your energy?

- ☐ What projects have you been able to spend hours on without tiring out?

- ☐ What are your hobbies and what do you like about them?

Once you've taken the time to honestly consider your strengths and weaknesses, you can move on to getting input from someone close to you whether it be a spouse, mentor, or close friend.

TALK TO OTHERS

You shouldn't end your list with just what you've put on it since you will most likely have a biased opinion of yourself. People tend to either think too much or too little of their own abilities; either they believe they know everything there is to know about a subject, or they hold themselves back with extreme scrutiny.

This is why you will need someone close to you who can help you see clearly and get closer to the truth about yourself. Choose three to five people who have been with you for an extended period of time, who have seen your behavior and character in a variety of situations.

In addition to the length of time you've known the person, you'll also want to make sure you trust and value their opinion. Avoid choosing someone who is too biased or likely to tell you only what you want to hear.

Instead, opt for people who are helpful and balanced, and have only ever been honest to you without being cruel. After you know who you want to talk to for this task, approach them and ask for their feedback. Keep an open mind and understand nothing may be fully accomplished in this life without constructive criticism and improvement.

When you approach them, tell them why you are asking for their opinion. Ask them what attributes you have that will add to your success. Also, ask them what your weaknesses are that can cause your business to fail.

As people give you feedback, you can refine and add detail to your two lists. You may confirm some of your strengths and weaknesses, while you make also find items that were on the wrong list or that you hadn't thought of before. After you've refined your lists you're ready to move on to the third step.

PERSONALITY TESTING

Once you've examined yourself and gained feedback from others, consider an unbiased third-party view of your strengths and weaknesses. Consider taking a personality test to see any other possibilities you agree or disagree with. There are a few different options to choose from when it comes to a testing platform.

Myers-Briggs Type Indicator (MBTI)

The MBTI is the go-to option for most corporate-level businesses. This test measures you in four framework areas: energy (introvert versus extrovert), decision-making, information intake, and your approach to the world around you.

You can either choose to pay $49.95 to take the official test, or you can do a similar test called the Jung Personality Test for free.

DISC Personality Testing

This is another popular test for corporations. This test determines the type of person you are and how you can best relate to others. You can choose between a free assessment and a full version for $29.

When you combine these broad personality tests with the finer details you gain from a self-assessment and others, you'll have a pretty good view of your strengths and weaknesses, as well as those talents you have yet to develop.

EXPERIMENT WITH NEW THINGS

Perhaps one of the most difficult things about identifying strengths and weaknesses is a lack of experience. For example, you may find that most weaknesses come down to something you've never tried.

Maybe you're reluctant to try new things, or you just haven't pushed yourself to do those activities before. If you want to try something new and broaden your list of abilities, consider some of the following.

CREATIVE ACTIVITIES

Consider trying painting and/or drawing. There are plenty of YouTube tutorials to help get you started. With just a few supplies you can easily try this one from the comfort of your own home and determining what types of paints you like.

I personally discovered I prefer drawing in grayscale using pencils than I do with watercolors or pastels. I have yet to try acrylics or ceramic, but it is still one of my goals to attempt it and see where those two take me.

Now, I learned from experience that I am no good at dancing, but if you had found yourself being adept at it, you could take a dance class or a few YouTube tutorials to improve your technique. You can start in your own home and as you get more practice and comfort, branch out to dance classes with other people.

If you enjoy photography, you could limit it just to that and nurture that ability, or you could take it up a notch and create a short movie. With modern technology, you have everything you need to make a high-quality film from your home computer, a tablet, or your phone.

Start by creating a 15 to 30-second clip that gets an emotional response from others, and you'll be able to learn a skill that can benefit you when marketing your business. You could try Claymation or stop-motion and develop a portfolio if you find you love using those techniques.

Leaving it at just photography could lead to you selling your professional-grade prints, or receiving commissions for big events like weddings or birthdays.

You could even try cooking from an online recipe or a cookbook you bought but have yet to use. Make a meal you've enjoyed at a restaurant or simply experiment with ingredients you like. Perhaps you find you are no good at cooking meat, but you make some killer pastries.

Regardless of what you use it on, this skill may help you create meals or sweet treats for those around you while saving money in the process. If you have a knack for baking and decorating cakes, not only could you share that with your friends and family, but also make your business out of it. Or if you become adept at making chocolate truffles or candy, that is another creative mine you can exploit for the better.

TECHNICAL SKILLS

A great activity to try that can greatly help with starting a business is website design and coding. You can watch tutorials or take classes from online sites like Codeacademy, or at your local community college, it all depends on the level of skill you want to gain.

For something simple, use a template service like Wix or take classes to learn the basic skills and design your own comprehensive website.

Also, consider taking the free online course for Google's Digital Analytics Fundamentals. This will help you get an idea of how your business website can work better than others.

FINANCIAL TOOLS

It can be a good idea to learn some financial skills before starting a business. Not only can it help you learn about saving, but it can help you learn how to manage the finances of your business.

Consider learning about investing and start with small investments so you can begin saving up money for your business startup. There are several apps out there that can help you invest with very little money.

Also, make sure to take a course or read up on budgeting. Having a personal and business budget can go a long way to making sure you don't overspend and have your business fail due to lack of cash flow.

Doing these things will teach you valuable skills for starting and running your business, and will also help you identify areas that you are already strong in and areas where you won't be able to perform even with training and experience. Once you've tried any of these areas, consider asking yourself the following questions:

- ☐ Was the experience enjoyable?

- ☐ What did you enjoy about it?

- ☐ What didn't you enjoy about it?

☐ Was the experience easy or difficult?

☐ Is it something you want to do again or something you can improve?

☐ If it was difficult for you, were you motivated to continue?

EVALUATE THE LISTS

Now that you've identified both your innate strengths and weaknesses, you can evaluate them for ones that may need extra attention. Some of your strengths may be the best you can do, and others will need a little extra effort.

Still, other skills won't even be too important to the success of your business. For instance, if you are great at making cupcakes, but you want to start a candle-making shop, there is not a real correlation between both skill sets.

When it comes to your weaknesses, some of them will be obvious. Weaknesses linked to your business should be addressed and improved in order to succeed. If the weaknesses aren't linked to your business, then you don't need to worry about them right now.

Now you'll have a good idea of what types of businesses in a general sense are good for you to undertake, and those that you should avoid. It is now time to start focusing on where to go for your business ideas and how to get started on the brainstorming portion of the process.

9 WAYS TO SEARCH FOR NEW BUSINESS IDEAS

There are a few places you can go for ideas. Make sure to look everywhere, since new trains of thought can come from the strangest of places, especially those you never even thought of in the first place.

Smartphones

This can be a great tool, particularly if you are looking to create an app. Take a look through the app store to see if any ideas spark. Search within categories that interest you and see if there is anything missing or see if there are apps that can be improved upon. You may have an idea in short order.

Search Engines

We have at our fingertips so much knowledge available from all over the world, and we rarely use it for more than watching cute animal videos. Instead, you can search for any product or service that comes to mind to see what already exists.

If you search for something but can't find it, perhaps you're onto a great business idea. If you find what you were looking for, but the top results can be improved upon, then you may be able to build upon an already-existing business plan.

Social Media

People on social media will often point out issues with products or services, allowing you to come up with a profitable solution. If you are not too keen on using social media platforms, you can comb through online review sites to find out where customers are dissatisfied and come with a business idea that improves upon this.

The World around You

Always take the time to pay attention to society and the world around you. There is no shortage of areas where you can come up with ideas for a business. Where you work, where you shop, even your home offers business ideas. Look at things you interact with on a daily basis and see if there is a solution you can offer.

Business ideas can truly come from anywhere. Once you have some new thoughts in mind, there are a few questions you have to ask yourself to evaluate if you have something you can make a profit out of on your own.

Is There a Solution to a Problem?

The best business ideas are those that address an existing problem. If you have experienced the problem firsthand or if you know of one that exists for more than a handful of people, you can come up with a solution that will turn into a profitable business.

Are You Good at It?

Do people constantly come to you to do something that is the basis for your business idea? If so, it can be a good branch for you. Basing a business around something you already have a talent for not only speeds up the learning curve, but it also grants you time to focus on other parts of your business.

What Do Others Say?

Do other people recognize a hidden talent in you? Have people told you to do something for a business? Take the time to think about something people have noticed in you, and put your own abilities to the test of having to do them with a time crunch.

For example, if you can sew beautiful patterns on dresses, but it takes you a few months to accomplish a single one, you may need to either improve upon your technique or find another ability to work with. Otherwise, taking months to deliver a single order will not be as profitable in the end.

What Services Are Lacking?

This is a popular area for business ideas. Have you ever looked for something specific and been unable to find it? Perhaps a thorough botany dictionary where you can take photos of an unknown plant, and it will be matched to one in the system in a matter of seconds.

Or applying the same concept to an unknown food when you are traveling abroad. Find a service that is lacking in something, and consider how you can turn that into a profitable business

Do You Make Something That Can Sell?

Lastly, consider what you do for a hobby or craft; is it something that people are willing to buy? If so, can you market it on a larger platform? There are plenty of e-commerce sites that allow you to sell handmade items. So, you must definitely consider the options available for starting a business selling items you make from home or a rented studio if you are working with more complicated or larger supplies.

By this point, you should have a list of some pretty viable business ideas. Now you need to test these ideas to narrow them to the few or single business that you should start.

Testing Your Business Idea

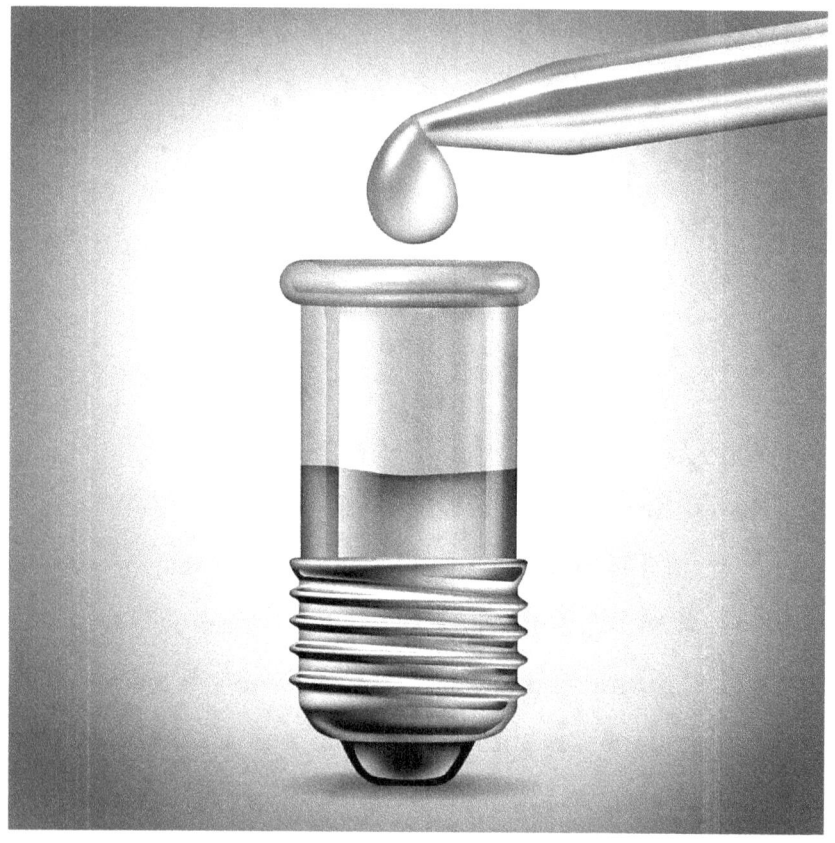

It can be a challenge to determine which business ideas to pursue, which to wait for a better time, and which should stay as a hobby. For one, you'll want to make sure you choose one that is worth your time and money.

While you can choose to go with your gut reaction, this can also be a good way to lead to business failure if you do not have the proper plan behind that feeling. Since most businesses fail within the first five years, you must take a few extra steps to ensure you have a well-developed structure of what you want to do before choosing to get started.

Let's look at how you can test your business idea before we move on to the steps for starting your actual business.

KEY BUSINESS ASSUMPTIONS

When you are first considering an idea, don't come up with a detailed business plan. Instead, write down the basic components of your idea, or the skeleton of it, if you will. Cover the following to help you see how well the plan will work:

- Why are you considering this business idea and what is your main mission?

- Every business is going to need a sense of purpose, so what is yours?

- Is the business solving some type of problem?

- Who is the business focused on serving?

- What competition stands between you and a thriving business?

- What makes your business a better option than the competition?

- Lastly, how confident are you that the business can make money?

- What are the overall financial forecasts for the business?

When you write down this general overview, you want to be quick. Only take about 30 minutes or less to write down your thoughts and comments.

Ideally, you'll only have about a page of information. This will give you the key assumptions of your business, and the rest of the process for testing your idea will see how accurate these assumptions are.

POTENTIAL CUSTOMERS

Many people with a new business idea often pass up the crucial step of talking with potential customers. Not doing this can greatly increase your chance of failure, so you need to talk to people in order to validate assumptions that you made while brainstorming. Is there really a problem to be addressed, and does your business idea really provide a solution?

Talk to as many people as possible so you can get multiple points of view–making a survey could speed up this process by a couple of days since you could ask more people in a shorter period of time.

If it is relevant to your idea, and if you have prior permission, visiting people's workplaces and getting a quick walkthrough will give you an insight into the decision-making process of that location. As you gain this insight, go back home when you are ready and adjust your ideas.

Make a Prototype If Possible

If your business idea includes an actual item, consider having a prototype made, or make one yourself out of cheaper ingredients. If you want to work with a small solid piece for a game or an art piece, you could make your own silicone mold of whatever it is you want and fill it with resin.

On the other hand, if you can't make a prototype, try to have at least images of what your final product will look like.

The goal is to let people see what you have to offer so they can critique your idea. The more real the item is, the better the quality of the feedback you'll get from potential customers.

DETERMINE HOW MUCH PEOPLE WILL PAY

As you get feedback from potential customers, also try to determine how much they will be willing to pay. This can be difficult since everyone is likely to want things for as close to free as possible. There are some things you can do other than coming out and asking directly.

First, if there are competitors, take a look at their pricing and determine what makes your company different. Another option is to look at the value that you are providing to the customer and base your price on that.

Once you have a price in mind, ask your potential customers if they would order your product or service for that price. People will often give you feedback if they don't feel the price is right. With this, you'll be able to determine if a customer thinks the price is fair or if they think you are asking for too much.

Now, remember to ask people who are not biased, but rather who fit the market you are aiming for. Only then will you have customers who understand the value of the service you are going to offer. You are not going to sell meat-based products to the community's group of vegans now, are you?

So, always ensure you have a target market in mind that covers age, geographic efficiency, and something those people have in common in terms of their job, economic status, or family structure.

DETERMINE STARTUP COSTS

As you talk to potential customers and refine your idea, you'll likely be getting closer to a more solid business plan, which ensures your chances of success. What you need to do next is to make sure your plan is financially viable with your current influx of money.

We'll go into more depth on this later, but at this stage, you'll want to have at least a rough estimate of the minimum amount needed to start the business and a realistic expectation of whether or not you can achieve the goal.

BE FLEXIBLE

While you are getting all this feedback, it is important to stay flexible. This doesn't mean you need to make adjustments every time you get a single opinion, but you want to pay attention to trends in opinions and adjust your overall plan to meet the needs of as many potential customers as possible to help your business afloat.

You may even be able to determine which customers are a permanent part of your target audience and which ones aren't. You can also get information on how to adjust your marketing and pricing once you start your business.

Now that you have tested your business plan, you've likely developed a strong series of steps that may or may not be vastly different from what you originally planned. You are now almost ready to start putting your business idea into action.

There are four things you need to do first, however, so pay close attention and bear with me for a minute.

With all the bits and pieces of having a target market, finding the holes in your original plan and fixing them, and setting an estimated price range for your products or services, you are deeper in this than you probably originally expected.

So, let's get into the specifics of what you need to do now.

MAKE THE DECISION TO START

When I first started my business, I was more of a mess than anything. I developed a few prototypes before understanding whether there was a market for them or not and nearly ran out of money half-way through the first few steps. It took me a while to take it easy and assess what I was doing with an objective mind.

Once I got a concrete skeleton of what I needed to do and spoke to several people in the market I was interested in selling to, everything got a lot smoother from there. I say this from experience: be patient, be organized, and understand this process takes time. A great business does not happen overnight, and its success depends on the work you are willing to put into it.

Vacations, hobbies, and your day job—you must work through all of these and eventually give a few of them up while you are creating the building blocks for a new business. Any bit of free time you have after your day job, you need to dedicate at least two hours into your plans.

If you have any doubts, take the time to write them down into a list. You may be surprised to find that most of the reasons on the list are limited only by yourself. It is important that you identify these and address them before you get your business started. Otherwise, these issues can make it difficult to turn your business into a success. Do this by thinking of an affirmative answer to each of the doubts on your life.

Often, you'll find that doubts around starting a business fall into one of two categories:

1. Lack of belief in yourself and/or your ability to succeed.

2. Fear of failure.

FURTHER DEVELOP YOUR IDEA AND MIND

Once you've overcome your fears, you can start moving forward. You'll need a lot of discipline in order to start your business, so you need to be focused, keep track of your progress, and make sure you take a new step towards improvement each day.

Even if it doesn't seem like you make any changes, be patient. Having small victories every day and doing the workload in separate chunks will eventually culminate to a solid platform of success.

In the early stages of starting your business, do everything you can to learn about your product, industry, competition, and technology to help increase your learning curve.

Now you have a strong idea, and you're determined to get your business off the ground and have it be a booming success.

So let's get started. The first step in the process is to come up with a strong business plan, which seems a bit redundant, but it is more concrete than a business idea.

The business plan is the guide or roadmap for your business. It sets goals and achievements as well as checkpoints to achieve those goals. There is a lot of work that goes into a business plan. So let's take a look at what you need.

What Is a Business Plan?

The simple act of writing down your business ideas is nearly the same as writing your business plan; it contains the same basic components. At its basic counterpart, a business plan is a layout of how your business will work and how you plan to have your business succeed.

Business Plan Length

A business plan is obviously going to be longer than a list of business ideas, but the actual length is going to vary by what you want to cover and what your plan is going to be used for. For most businesses, you'll only need a simple lean plan that contains a few bullet points to focus your strategy, tactics, milestones, and basic financial projections.

Revising Business Plans

The most important part of a business plan is the reviewing and revising the schedule. At specific times you should review your business progress and how many goals you've achieved.

When reviewing, you want to measure your milestone progress against your actual progress and financial projections. You can then make revisions as needed to set new and more realistic goals.

TYPES OF BUSINESS PLANS

There are three main types of business plans you can choose to use. Let's look at these types of business plans and which ones should be used.

SINGLE-PAGE PLAN

This is just what it sounds like: a brief summary of your business in a single page. The key with this plan is to describe your business in concise terms that is to-the-point and direct. There are two purposes for this type of business plan. For one, it is a great way to introduce your business to others, such as potential investors.

Most investors don't have time to read detailed 40-paged plans so that a single page can be an easier, cleaner, more professional approach. You may need a more detailed alternative later, but this is a great way to get started.

In addition, the single-page plan is good for new companies that simply wish to broadly describe their business idea. In this case, the business plan is basically an expanded version of writing down your ideas. This option allows you to see the entire concept and quickly refine things as your idea changes.

THE LEAN PLAN

This is a slightly more detailed business plan than the single page and provides more financial information. However, it still isn't as long or involved as the traditional business plan. The lean plan is typically used for internal strategic planning and growth.

It doesn't focus on the formalities needed when presenting your plan for investment and rather focuses on more internal needs such as strategy, tactics, milestones, budgets, and forecasts.

A lean plan is going to skip sections such as company history and management team since everyone within the company is likely to know all this. It also won't have an exit strategy section since you aren't presenting it to investors.

The best lean plan uses bullet points to define a business strategy and tactics with specific dates and tasks, as well as essential numbers such as projected sales, spending, and cash flow. The ideal lean plan will be about five to ten pages, all of which should be reviewed and revised at least once a month.

THE STANDARD PLAN

The standard business plan is designed for people unrelated to the operation of the business to read and learn about what said business is all about. A standard or full business plan is typically used to convince investors to provide funding and to support the application for a business loan.

Sometimes this plan can also be used to recruit or train employees, but it isn't common unless you need an extra pair of hands in the long run for larger-scale business growth.

The standard business plan is an extension of the internal plan or the lean business plan. This sort needs to be polished and well documented, with very close attention to detail, language, and format. It also needs to show how potential funds are going to be used, as well as a strong emphasis on the team that is starting the company.

Investors prefer to look at the people rather than the idea and need to know how the individuals are going to help the company grow and become successful. We'll look into the details of writing this type of plan in a moment. First, let's consider the five things you need to do before writing your chosen style of a business plan.

FIVE THINGS TO DO BEFORE WRITING A BUSINESS PLAN

There is a lot involved in starting a new business and being prepared for all the steps that can make the process easier. One of the best ways to increase your chances of being prepared for your business is to have a solid business plan.

The standard information and the technical aspects are easy to do, but the abstract part consists of things you need to figure out before you start to write your business plan. To have better success when writing this, you should do five things in preparation.

Define a Purpose

It is important to identify and describe your business' core values and purpose. Having a purpose helps provide your business with direction so you can make decisions at all levels based on which course of action to take.

Develop Your Vision

The key to a successful business is to have a clear vision of what the business is going to accomplish. To do this, you need to have three to five key strategies that will help you reach your goals. Along with this, you need to have a clear mission statement or the why of what your business is doing.

The second most important thing is your "value proposition" which defines what makes your business unique within your chosen marketplace and how you intend to make your business different from others.

Have a Clear Business Model

Having a clear financial business model is important when it comes to placing details in your formal business plan. This includes hiring, pricing, sales, cost of acquisition, expenses, and growth.

The business plan needs to be reviewed and updated as the business develops and grows, and to stay organized it is best to update it every week, or every two weeks if it is going slow at first.

DETERMINE YOUR TARGET MARKET

This can be one of the more difficult steps. Ask yourself why you are offering your product or service and who is interested in it. Then ask why you are attracted to this type of client. Make sure you have a clear definition of who you are dealing with.

TEST YOUR IDEA

You've likely already done this step, but if not, you need to get out and talk to experts, potential customers, or anyone within your target market to determine the viability of your idea.

Simply writing your business plan isn't going to mean your business will be an automatic success, but it does help provide a map to how you'll get there. The more effort you put into writing your business plan, the easier it will be to track your progress and see which areas you still lack in, or which ones you can relax about.

WRITING A BUSINESS PLAN STEP-BY-STEP

Plan   Run

Write a plan.
Run the plan.
Review the plan.
Revise the plan.
Repeat.

Revise   Review

Let's take a look at each part of a standard business plan and the details you need to include in every section mentioned.

EXECUTIVE SUMMARY

This section of your business plan is designed to introduce your company, explain what you do, and describe what you are looking for from readers. It is going to be the first chapter of your business plan and is often best written last, ironically enough, since writing the rest of the business plan first will allow you to know all the details of the said business and better prepare you to write this area.

It is easy to write a summary of a book after you know what the book is about, right? So, it is with that same logic that we come back to this portion after you have taken care of the other pages.

You should write an executive summary with a view toward creating a stand-alone document that highlights the details of your business plan. Some investors may even ask solely for the executive summary when evaluating a business potential. If your executive summary is well-written, then the investor may ask to see the complete business plan and rest of your data.

Because of this important nature, you want the executive summary to be clear and concise. It should cover the key highlights of your business without going into too much detail. The executive summary should be one to two pages long and intrigue people into wanting to read more.

The Important Components You Must Include

Single Sentence Overview

At the top of the page, directly below your business name, you need to have a single sentence overview of your business. This should sum up what your business is doing, basically, as well as what it intends to accomplish in the long-run. This is also known as your value proposition.

Problem

In one to two sentences, you should describe the problem you are solving within your market.

Solution

This is where you talk about your product or service. Tell how you are addressing the problem you have just described.

Target Market

Describe your ideal customer, and how many of those exist. You want to be very specific in the type of market segment you are targeting. This will make it easier to define your marketing strategies later on, and why they would work will be fairly self-explanatory.

COMPETITION

What current products or services are currently in place to solve the problem today? Are there alternatives to what you are offering or substitutes? Every business is going to have some level of competition, and you need to provide an overview of this in your executive summary segment.

Address the competition, and explain why they pose no major threats to your business, or what makes yours stand out from the others.

TEAM

Briefly describe your team and provide a short description of why you and your team are the right people for the market you are trying to reach. Investors focus heavily on the team, sometimes more than the idea itself, since you need to execute your idea to have the business become a reality, and a trustworthy group of people are what will get you to that finish line.

FINANCIAL SUMMARY

Highlight the main areas of your financial plan. Ideally, you should have a chart with planned sales, expenses, and profitability. This is also the area to provide additional explanation of your business model if needed. If there is a predicted slow growth, make sure you mention it.

FUNDING REQUIREMENTS

If you want to raise money to start your business, you'll need to include details of what you need within your executive summary.

Don't set terms for a potential investment since you'll negotiate this later. Instead, just place a short statement about how much money you need to raise to get your business started, and the options you have to acquire it.

MILESTONES AND TRACTION

The last main element of the executive summary that investors want to see will be depicted here, including the progress you've made and the future milestones you intend to reach. This is a great spot to highlight any customer interest in what you have to offer and/or any presales you've made.

If you are writing a lean business plan, you can skip this executive summary or at least greatly reduce it by limiting the details of the management team, funding requirements, and tractions.

Take this opportunity to just use the executive summary as an overview of the direction your company is going so that everyone involved in the business is on the same page to start.

Opportunity

This is the most important part of your business plan, which is the culmination of everything we have mentioned before, but with clean paragraphs. Here you will describe in detail what problem or issue you are solving, what your solution is, who you plan to target, and how your product or service meets the existing market and competition.

In this section, you'll also want to show what sets you apart from the competition and how you plan to expand your business in the future. Those who are reading your plan will already know a little about your idea from the executive summary.

However, this chapter is going to expand the initial overview and give more details while answering questions that aren't covered in the executive summary.

PROBLEM AND SOLUTION

This chapter should be started by describing the existing problem that you plan to solve. Discuss how the problem is currently being dealt with and how your product or service is different. Is your option cheaper, easier, or closer to your target audience?

Determining the problem is the most important part of a business plan and is key to the success of your business. If you can point to a specific problem customers have, then you are more likely to have a viable business idea.

After identifying the problem, the next step is to describe your solution. This is the very detailed description of your product or service you plan to offer to the customer. What are you offering? Be specific. How exactly are you going to solve the problem you've just described?

Once you have finished describing the problem and solution, you want to start focusing on your target market or the people you will be selling to. Depending on your business idea and the type of business plan you are trying to write, you may not need to provide a whole lot of detail here.

At the least, you do need to know who your target customer is and approximately how large that number is all together. If there aren't enough customers, this can be a warning sign of an unsuccessful business idea, or perhaps an invitation to modify it in such a way that it is more accessible.

If you plan to do a formal market analysis, you'll need to do some research. First, you'll need to identify your market segments.

Next, you'll need to determine how big each of these segments is. For the sake of definition, a market segment is a specific group of people or other businesses that you are able to sell to.

As important as offering a specific product or service, you have to detail who you will market and sell to. The first thing to do is describe your market. Not just who you are selling to, but how many are there, and who else is doing the same thing as you want to do.

That is what market analysis is. We need to talk about the basics of market segmentation, then discuss the questions you will need to answer in this section.

EVALUATION OF THE MARKET

Your market is not everyone. Therefore, your market research and analysis have the goal of identifying your market segments. A segment is a group of people within your market that will buy your product or service. Each of the segments is your target market.

Out of everyone, there are specific groups that will buy your product or service. In the example of Bubba's, the market segments are:

- Families
- Couples
- Groups of friends
- Individuals

Each segment will have a percentage of who dines out, where, when, and why. Are they looking for a specific kind of food, theme, atmosphere or convenience of location? Will they use the drive-through window? What is the average age and the average amount of the ticket?

A good business plan not only identifies the target market, but it also breaks it down into segments and includes data showing how fast each will grow from many angles. Here is the methodology:

TAM: Total Available Market. How big is the entire market that you could provide product or service to? For instance, the entire city Bubba's is located in has a population of three million people.

SAM: Segmented Available Market. The group you will target from the TAM data. For instance, Bubba's will be on the east side of the main county of the city. That area of town's population is 650,000 people plus 45,000 college students who are in residence nine months a year.

SOM: Share of Market. This subset is who you could actually reach in the first year or so of being in business. This number is extrapolated from SAM. How many of those 650,000 people and the 45,000 college students can you reach and convince to spend their money on your product?

While you are putting together the numbers and size of your market segments, also research the potential growth of each. Does the college market segment basically stay the same year to year? How many students remain in the area? How fast is the target area of 650,000 growing per year, in percentages? Is it in decline?

The growth or decline must be in relation to the population of the market segment. For instance, the population of the 650,000-person area may be growing 3% a year. What are those changes and why are they happening?

Are more families appearing in the mix; a higher number of teenagers or millennials; retired people; high salaries, lower; what is the trend of the neighborhoods?

Research topics to visit, such as:

- Bubba's is in a residential neighborhood, great schools and a mix of salary ranges. Address what the salary levels are. Number of schools, grade levels, attendance.
- There are apartment complexes. What kind, who lives there, economic view, children, students, etc.
- Level of various ethnics in the entire area. For example, will Orientals eat barbeque? Is this a pocket of ethnicity? Much like a Little Italy or Little Viet Nam?
- Single family homes. Price range, number, and age of homes. Turnover of the real estate, etc.

- Large shopping area. How many restaurants, what type; clothing or grocery stores, what audience; movie theaters, how many?

- Traffic distribution system. Close to main arteries, easy access for others in the city, the main drag?

- What other businesses are in the area? Is there an airport, hotels, hospitals?

- Reaching your market and creating profits is limited by all the other businesses in the industry. You have to find ways to overcome those limits.

KEY CUSTOMERS

The last section dealing with the target market is going to focus on your key customers. This area is only needed if your company is going to have very limited customers with special necessities. Most companies will end up selling to all consumers and won't need this area.

If you are selling to other businesses, you may have a few key customers that are necessary to your business' success. If this is the case, you'll need to use this area to provide

details about these customers and why they are of utmost
importance.

EVALUATION OF THE COMPETITION

If you are opening a restaurant, what other and how many
restaurants are in your marketing area? What are the
sizes, are they a chain, what are the themes, what are the
foods served and what audience to they attract? What are
their hours, do they deliver?

If you want a shop to sell clothes, whose clothes are you
selling? Just baby, just women or men, teenagers, sports,
family? Who are the competitors? For instance, how well
would a boutique shop do against a Kohl's or Target?
Would the neighborhood support it, or would word of
mouth? Are you different enough and how?

When you discuss the competition, talk about who is
offering the same services or providing the same products.
Other businesses want to solve your customer's problems,
too. How is what you are going to offer better? What is
your advantage? Discuss how, in your environment, you
will create a better, more successful business. This is also
called the value proposition.

Business people typically use a competitor matrix to list competitors and how they stack up against themselves. Build your matrix using excel if it will be a long comparison chart. If not, or if you prefer, just build it in chart form in Word.

List you and your competitors down the left side. This is column one. Build additional columns next to it listing each of the competitor's features.

Name	Casual	Late hrs.	7 Days	Lit	Easy in-	Street	Other and
	or	Reg.	or Days	Parking	out	View or	and Food Served
	Theme	Hours	Open	Lot	Access	any View	
Friday's							
Chili's							
Fridays							
Mac Grill							

MacDonald					
Panera Bread					
Red Lobster					
Shake and Steak					

This is just a slice of an example. Use multiple columns for every amenity and as many competitors as possible. Have layout and printing done professionally if conceivable. Regardless of size, the chart must be professional for a business plan presented to investors.

Evaluation of Market Characteristics

As part of an industry, your readers, investors, need to understand the market of your industry. Not everyone knows about the carpet or home improvement industry, food or technology industries. But, you need to, and you have to explain it clearly, knowledgeably and concisely.

Discuss a little of the history of the industry, profitability and the health of the overall industry. Think about steel. You are probably not going into that industry but think about the history you could write. From the industrial revolution to foreign trade and tariffs. You don't have to write a book, but put together several paragraphs or a timeline pointing out the milestones.

What are the trends? For instance, do people prefer marble, tile and wood floors instead of wall to wall carpet in every room? Why, who are these people, and what is their price point? People dress more casually today than in the past. Where is that trend/style now, why did it change, will it continue, and why?

Sports equipment changes, cooking trends, even the automobiles that we own. Changes can be due to changes in the market such as availability and/or imports, tariffs, or changes in trends. Life changes affect a product or service, for instance, aging, marriage, children, college, retirement, and so on.

You may be thinking that these descriptions and history are too big or too much for you, simply extend the application, extrapolate.

For instance, sports equipment. The history of biking is manageable. And, your little shop could handle repairs of the new and/or foreign bikes. Performance bikes, road, mountain, carbon fiber, Bianchi, Schwinn, and high-tech components. Whatever you want to target, and possibly include biking groups and biking excursions.

Here is another simpler example. A sports shoe or equipment store could offer custom orthodontics that are at sky-rocket prices at podiatrists. You have heard of diving goggles with prescription lenses. Where would a diver find those? Do you have a dive shop? Partner with local eye doctors. Are you selling surfboards, excursions, lessons?

Another example. What trends have the auto and auto repair industries gone through? What is up ahead? The new high-tech cars need specific technical training for repairs. Cameras on the four sides may be damaged with just a bump to the car. Repairs for the future high-tech automobiles is going to be expensive.

It is going to be a long time before you can buy parts for this sensitive equipment on Amazon or a parts department or store. Maybe you could be the local service professional person for repairs listed on Amazon.

All of the new technology like cameras, devices, giggles, and gaggles' repairs will be extremely high and extremely profitable. Beware of products that are cheap to replace instead of repair.

The kind of in-depth facts and data I am telling you to obtain and clearly state is the data that proves there is a market for your product or service. It is also the basis of your forecasted sales, states that there is a future, and how far can you take your expertise.

The facts and data determine the size of your business and practically write your marketing plan for you. This research identifies your financial needs and anticipated profits.

INTO THE FUTURE

Everyone who starts a business has an idea of where they want to go in the future once they become successful. While it can be tempting to put a lot of thought and work into the expansion of your business, you don't want to go into too much detail on this in your business plan.

It is enough just to have a paragraph or two about what your plans are for the future, so investors know where you are headed. The main focus of the business plan needs to be on your products and services that you have to offer the market right now.

EXECUTION

Once you've finished with the opportunity chapter, you'll need to move on to describe in detail how your business is actually going to work. During this section, we will cover the marketing and sales plans, operations, success measurements, and the milestones you want to achieve.

MARKETING AND SALES PLANS

This section of your business plan describes how you will reach your target market segments, how you plan to sell to them, what your pricing plan is, and the types of activities and partnerships you require to make your business a success.

Before you can write this section of your business plan, you'll need to have a well-defined target market and have a good description of your buyer persona(s). A marketing plan won't have much value if you don't have a clear understanding of who you are marketing to, so please try the survey idea and take a few days to fully have the answers for this portion.

Doing it in a rush will not only give you incomplete results, but it will also hinder the rest of your process.

POSITIONING

The first stage of your marketing plan needs to discuss how you are positioning your company and the product or service you are offering. Positioning is how you'll be presenting your company to prospective customers.

Before developing a positioning statement, it is a good idea to evaluate the current market and answer the following questions:

- What benefits or features do you offer that are different from your competitors?

- What are the needs and/or wants of your customers?

- What is the positioning of your customers?

- How do you plan on standing out from the competition?

- Why would a customer choose you over the competition?

- Where is your company positioned among the other solutions being offered?

After you've taken the time to answer these questions, then you'll be able to come up with a positioning statement and define it within your business plan. This statement doesn't have to be long and overly detailed.

Simply state where your company lies within the competitive landscape and what makes you different from the others offering the same or similar solutions. So, nothing that we have not done before, as you can see.

PRICING

After you have defined your positioning strategy, you can start focusing on price. Your positioning strategy will have a big impact on how your product or service is priced. Price sends a message to your customers and can help communicate your position to them.

Often deciding on a price is more art than science, but you should follow the following basic rules:

1. Cover your costs.

While there are exceptions to this, you generally want to be charging people more than it costs you to actually deliver the product or service.

2. Primary and secondary pricing.

The initial price you charge may not be the primary source of profit. The maintenance or support for the product may be the primary source of profit, on the other hand.

3. Market rate.

Lastly, your prices should match up with demand and expectations of customers. If you price too high, you won't have customers, and if you price too low, you won't have people valuing what you're offering. It is all about finding that happy balance and not going overboard on either side.

There are three strategies you can use when it comes to pricing your product or services.

- Cost-Plus Pricing. It involves looking at your costs then marking up appropriately. This is effective if you are manufacturing a product and need to cover initial costs.

- Market-Based Pricing. Where we look at the price set by competitors, then basing your price on what the market is expected to be. You establish your position within the market by choosing to price on the high or low end depending on the personal cost you are putting into your services.

- Value Pricing. This method involves pricing based on the value and quality of product or service you are providing to customers.

PROMOTION

Once you have finished with positioning and pricing, you can start to look at your promotion strategy. This part of the plan will provide details on how you will communicate with your customers.

It is important to measure how much your promotions costs compared to how many sales you gain. If a promotional program isn't profitable, it can be difficult to maintain it for the long-term.

5 KEY AREAS CONSIDER FOR YOUR MARKETING PLAN

There are a few different areas that you want to consider when writing out your promotional plan:

PACKAGING

When selling a product, the packaging is critical. If you have images, include them in your business plan. Having an actual prototype is even better if you have access to such a thing. The packaging section of your business plan needs to include the answers to the following questions:

- Is your packaging mirroring your positioning strategy?

- Does your packaging communicate your key value proposition?

- How does your packaging compare to that of the competition?

ADVERTISING

This needs to be an overview of the types of advertising your plan to pay for. Are you going to do most of your advertising online or will you also use traditional media? The key component to this section is the measurement of success for your advertising.

Public Relations

A great way to reach potential customers is media coverage. When you get a prominent review, it can give your business the exposure it needs to grow and be successful. If you plan to have a public relations strategy, you need to put the details in your business plan here.

Content Marketing

One of the more popular options for promotion is content marketing. This is what business plans are designed for, for the most part. This method is when you publish useful information for free, so your target market can learn about your company and the advice you can offer.

Social Media

Social media is becoming a requirement for many businesses. Now, that doesn't mean you need to be on all social media channels if you do not particularly want to manage all of them at the same time. You just need to be on the ones that your customers are most likely to be on as well.

STRATEGIC ALLIANCES

A part of your marketing plan may involve working closely with another company in the form of a partnership. This partnership can help you access a target market while allowing the partner company to offer their customers with a new product or service. If you already have a partnership established, you want to describe it here.

OPERATIONS

In this section, you will write about how your business works. This includes logistics, technology, and other details. Depending on what type of business you're starting, you may not need all of the following sections under this area. Simply include what you explicitly need and disregard the rest.

Sourcing and Fulfillment

If you are going to be buying products from vendors, then you need to include the details here, such as how you plan to deliver the products to customers.

Technology

While you don't need to give away trade secrets, you do need to describe how your technology is different and better than what the competition has to offer. You may need to describe how your technology works.

You don't need to include too much since investors will ask for additional details only if they need them. Remember the business plan needs to be as short as possible, since too much detail can make the plan too long, making it undesirable to read.

DISTRIBUTION CHANNELS

This portion of the business plan is important for product companies. In general, service companies can skip this area, since it focuses on how you plan to get your product into the hands of customers.

Distribution channels are unique to each industry, and the best way to come up with a plan for your distribution is to talk with others in the industry and determine what their distribution model is. There are a few common distribution models that you may want to consider:

DIRECT

This is your simplest and most profitable option. You can sell directly to your customers and pass the savings along to them, or you can increase your profit margins. You'll still need to describe the logistics of how you'll get products from your warehouse to customers, but this model is often the easiest to do and to keep up with.

RETAIL DISTRIBUTION

Often larger retailers won't want to deal with individual suppliers. Rather, they buy through distribution companies that sell products from a range of suppliers and make inventory available to retailers. These distributors will often take a percentage of sales that go through the warehouses.

MANUFACTURERS' REPRESENTATIVES

These are often salespeople who work for a "repping" agency. They work to sell your products to the right channels, in other words. They will often be on the job on commission and will typically help you get access to a distributor or retailer.

OEM

This means 'original equipment manufacturer.' If you sell your product to another company, then it uses your original prototype in their final item. This is the OEM channel.

Typically, companies will use a mix of distribution channels, so you don't need to limit yourself to just one single channel.

MILESTONES AND METRICS

In the grand scheme of things, your business plan is little to nothing more than a document. You need an implementation plan that includes a schedule, as well as defined roles and responsibilities.

While this section of your plan may not be too long, it is important that you look forward to the next crucial steps in starting your business. Investors prefer to see that you know what needs to happen in order to start your business and that you have a realistic schedule.

Start by doing a quick overview of your milestones. These are your planned major goals, which can be milestones related to prototypes, finding manufacturers, and receipts of the first order.

From the milestones, keep looking forward. You may also choose to look back if you've already had any major accomplishments. This is called traction by investors and means you are showing that your company has already had early success.

It can take the form of initial sales, a pilot program, or a partnership, so that you may give investors proof that your company is more than an idea on paper; it shows you are likely to be a successful and growing business.

METRICS

You also want to detail all key metrics that you'll be monitoring as your business grows. These are the numbers that you regularly view in order to determine the health status of your business.

If they have unfavorable 'symptoms,' it gets easier to find solutions on the spot and preventing a massive downfall or a major issue, for instance. Key metrics are what drive the growth of your business and your financial plan.

KEY ASSUMPTIONS AND RISKS

Lastly, your business plan needs to detail key assumptions that you create which are essential to the success of your business. You can also achieve that goal by thinking about risk. What risks come with starting your business?

The answer to that question can make the difference between a successful business and a failure, so long as you take them in mind with a realistic angle. The more you can minimize your assumptions, the more likely you will be to have a successful business.

TEAM BUILDING

Here we will focus on the structure of your company and who the key members are. These details are significant to investors because they want to know who is behind the company and how they can help the success of the business.

It is easier to help someone whose face you can see and whose lifestyle you can gauge out than a collection of nameless individuals with no detailed personalities.

LEADERSHIP

Investors often choose to invest in the people rather than the idea. This basically means that the investors want to be sure you can accomplish what you have planned, and make it to the next level while paying them back in full lat.

Do you have the right leadership in place to turn your idea into a successful business with interested customers? Do you need another hand to help you out in, or a mentor to handle the key aspects of the business first?

This chapter of your business plan is where you'll make your case that you have the right team to execute your business idea, as each member is qualified by your standards of experience or education to carry out their assigned task. It also shows investors that you've given thought to the roles and responsibilities your business needs in order to be successful.

We want to write down brief biographies of team members while highlighting their experience and education, or showing a portfolio if it one of them has more of a self-taught type of approach.

You want to focus on the reason why the team is the right one to start the business, and why you chose them specifically based on the quality of their performance. If you show you trust your team, it will justify their presence to the investors.

You don't need a complete management team to write a business plan. In fact, missing key people can be a sign of maturity and knowledge from an investment point of view. If you have gaps, identify them and show that you are looking for the right individuals to fill the roles, and how that will be addressed in due time based on salary and expectations.

Lastly, you may also want to show a proposed organizational chart in the plan. This isn't necessary, but you may be asked for it at some point to clarify certain concepts. An organizational chart can help raise money as well as be used to plan the growth of the company over time.

COMPANY

This is likely to be the shortest section of your business plan. In fact, if you are doing a lean plan that is used internally in your business, then you'll even be skipping this section. If you intend to share your business plan with others, though, you'll need to include the following:

- Mission Statement

- Intellectual Property

- Legal Structure and Ownership

- Business Location

- Brief History of Existing Company (If Applicable)

MISSION STATEMENT

You are likely to cover this area in just an hour or two with a couple of food breaks in between. The mission statement needs to be short, so no more than one or two well-versed sentences summarizing what you and your business are trying to do. Often, your mission statement might be the same as your overall value proposition.

INTELLECTUAL PROPERTY

This area will often only apply to technology and scientifically-inclined companies. If you don't need to discuss patents or other intellectual properties, you can skip this area altogether. If you do have intellectual property linked to your business, you'll want to write down key details of information for that part.

You should also highlight any patents or anything about a new bit of technology you want to implement in the application process. You should also disclose if you are licensing core technology from someone else, as well as any financial partnerships involved.

LEGAL STRUCTURE AND OWNERSHIP

You will need to include an overview of your current business structure. We'll discuss more about choosing this in a later chapter, so don't worry if we do not go too much into depth with it just yet.

You'll also want to provide an overview of how the business is owned. How is ownership divided if there are multiple owners? Most investors want to know this information before investing in a company, so they know what they are dealing with.

COMPANY HISTORY

If you have an existing company in place, you must include a brief history of it and highlight any achievements. This section should be no more than a few paragraphs in length. Writing down the history behind an existing company is a helpful tool when it comes to giving context to the rest of your present business plan, as well as your internal business plans.

It can also give new employees a background for the company they are hired by, giving them a clearer sense of what their jobs are.

BUSINESS LOCATION

Lastly, in this section, you should describe your current business location and any facilities you already own. This information is important if you are going to serve customers from a store. It can also be good for businesses that need manufacturing facilities, warehouses, or any other processing facilities.

FINANCES

The chapter we are about to read is particularly important, as it will give a structure to your financial plan for your business. This is often the most difficult part to write, but with a little planning, it can be easier.

The average financial plan will have monthly projections for the first 12 months of the business, then an annual projection for the next three to five years. For most startup businesses, a three-year projection is enough, but a few investors will want to see a five-year projection for a more thorough idea of the future of the company will be.

Let's look at what you need to include in this section for a great financial plan that will have investors impressed with your attention for detail and technicalities.

SALES FORECAST

This is exactly what it sounds like. It is a projection of how much you are going to sell over the next three to five years. This forecast is often divided into several rows, where each row focuses on a product or service you're offering. At this point, you are just giving a light surface forecast, and won't need to go into great detail.

You should also have a corresponding column for each sale row that covers the Cost of Goods Sold or COGS. These columns will show the expenses related to producing a product or delivering a service.

COGS will only include direct costs related to the product or service and not business expenses such as rent, insurance, salaries, or other premeditated figures.

PAYROLL

This plan needs to detail how and how much you will pay the employee. For small companies, you can list each position and their monthly amount. For a larger company, you'll need to break it down into functional groups.

You'll also want to cover what is termed 'employee burden' or the cost beyond salary per employee. This would be things such as payroll taxes, insurance, vacations, and other monthly costs that come with having an employee on the payroll.

PROFIT AND LOSS STATEMENT

Also referred to as an Income Statement, this is where all your numbers will come together to show if your business is making a profit or taking a loss. The profit and loss statement takes the data from your sales forecast and your personnel plan and places them all in a single place.

It contains the important bottom line where expenses are subtracted from earnings to determine if you will be making a profit each month or if you'll have some losses as you grow. A typical profit and loss spreadsheet will include the following:

- Sales

- COGS(Cost of Goods Sold)

- Gross Margin

- Operating Expenses

- Operating Income

- Interest, Taxes, Depreciation, and Amortization

- Total Expenses

- Net Profit

Cash Flow Statement

This statement is often confused with the profit and loss statement, but it is quite different and self-explanatorily, also has a different purpose. The cash flow statement tracks how much cash or money your business has in the bank at any point. The difference between these two statements is cash and profits.

Profit and loss will show a sale has been made, but you may not have access to the money from the payment for several days.

Most cash flow statements start with the amount of cash you have on hand. It will then add new cash through sales and paid invoices while subtracting cash paid out in the form of bills, loans, taxes, and other expenses. In the end, you'll have your total cash flow.

The cash flow statement is good to show you when you are low on cash, and when is the right time to purchase new equipment or other upgrades.

It is very helpful to show you how much you'll need to borrow or raise in order to grow your company since you will know when to go on saving-mode and when it is safe to make a few purchases for the improvement of your business.

BALANCE SHEET

The last financial statement you'll need to put together is the balance sheet. This shows an overview of your business' financial health. So, we will see what assets your company has as well as liabilities and equity from the owner(s).

Subtracting the liabilities from the assets will determine the net worth of the company, which is one of the more important parts you need to highlight.

USE OF FUNDS

If you plan to raise money from investors, you should include this brief section that details how you will use investors' money. You don't need to go into great detail, but you should show the major areas where the money will be spent.

This can be things like marketing, research, and development, sales, or even inventory purchases.

Exit Strategy

This is the final thing you want to include in your business plan. This is your plan for eventually selling the business either to another company or to the public as an IPO.

Investors require knowing your thoughts on this since they will want a return on their investment, and sometimes the only way to get this is through the sale of the company to someone else unless your company is making so much profit you can pay them back on your own without being acquired.

Again, you don't need a lot of details for this section, but you should identify companies that may be interested in buying your business if you are successful, or why you would not want to sell the company in the long run.

So that is all you need to come up with a strong and successful business plan. Let's move on to the next major part, which is coming up with the funds you need to start your business.

Business Funding

Starting a business isn't going to come cheap and determining your funding is an important and critical step. There are a lot of financial decisions you need to make when starting a business, including where you are going to get your startup funding.

In this chapter, we are going to look at how you can determine the amount of startup money you need, where to go for funding, and how to choose and get approved for small business loans.

ESTIMATING STARTUP COSTS

Starting a business is a wonderful prospect for many, but the process can be daunting. In addition to time and dedication, you're also going to need money to start your business.

So, before we look at where you can go for your financing, let's take the time to determine how much money you need in order to get your business started.

START SMALL

Anyone starting a new company is going to have high expectations. However, you want to take care that you don't invest too much too quickly. It is best to start small in the beginning and go into the venture with an open mind and prepare for any potential issues that may come up while starting your business.

To do this, you may want to test your product or service first as we described earlier. This way you can know whether people are interested and how much they are willing to pay.

MAKE AN ESTIMATE OF COSTS

Based on a study by the US Small Business Administration, the average microbusinesses costs $3,000 to start while most home-based businesses cost about $2,000 to $5,000 to start.

Each business has their own financing needs so there are some tips you can take that will allow you to determine how much cash you personally need to start your business.

First, you'll need at least six months of fixed costs. Don't underestimate expenses and keep in mind that they are likely to increase as the business grows. Consider the following costs.

One-Time versus Ongoing Costs

One-time expenses are those that are mostly done in the startup process. If there is a month when you need to make an equipment purchase, then you'll likely have more money going out than in for that month. You'll need to make up for this cash flow in the following month. On the other hand, ongoing costs are those paid out regularly, such as utilities. Costs like that are unlikely to change much from month to month.

Essential versus Optional Costs

Essential costs are those necessary to the growth and development of the company. Optional purchases are those that should only be made when the budget allows, and only after more urgent bills are paid.

Fixed versus Variable Costs

Fixed expenses like rent and utilities are the ones typically remain consistent from month to month. Variable expenses are those dependent on product or service sales. The burden of fixed costs is greater when a business first starts, but become less noticeable as the business grows.

Projected Cash Flow

You should project your cash flow for at least the first three months. It is best to add up fixed costs as well as estimated costs of goods and revenues for both best and worst case scenarios.

After you've determined the costs and come up with cash flow projections, you will want to consider how to get financed. Let's consider your funding sources.

Money is the ultimate life blood of any business. Without it you can't start or run any business. Before we get into some of the more conventional funding ideas, here are some basic ideas you should consider first.

1. Your own savings/401K etc.
2. Home equity line of credit (this is how I got started with mine)
3. Family funding (where your parents, siblings help you with a personal loan)
4. Create partnership with people that have the money
5. Credit cards cas advances (Be careful with this idea)

When it comes to choosing funding sources, they must match the needs of your company. We are going to discuss the six main sources of funding for business startups, and what each one entails.

After that point, you may go for the one you believe will work best for your personal situation and financial plan.

Venture Capital

This funding source is often misunderstood. Sometimes, people who are starting a business complain about how venture capital companies might not always be interested in assisting them with funds. However, it is important to note that venture capitals are no different from other businesses.

Those who work for a venture capital business are in charge of other people's money and need to be careful where they place their risk to make sure they choose a good risk/return ratio.

Therefore, venture capital is only a good source of funding for a specific few startup businesses. Venture capitalists won't invest in startups unless there is a good combination of product and market opportunity with proven management.

In other words, venture capitalists are only looking for businesses that can produce a huge increase in business within a few years so their investors will not raise an eyebrow at their decisions.

ANGEL INVESTMENT

This is one of the more common forms of investment for startup companies. While it is similar to venture capital, there are some important differences. Angel investors are typically groups or individuals who are investing their own money into an idea or business.

They also tend to only invest in businesses at the early stages, while venture capitalists wait until businesses have a few years of growth. Like venture capitalists, angel investors tend to focus on high-growth companies that are in the early stages.

CROWD FUNDING

This is one very popular way to get funding now a days. Crowd funding is essentially when you pitch your business idea to small investors either on or offline. If you want to explore this avenue, make sure you have a great business pitch ready then visit sites like:

- Kickstarter.com
- GoFundMe.com
- Indiegogo.com
- RocketHub.com

- GoGetFunding.com

As for offline crowdfunding, I have never tried it myself, but have seen people do it. You can make a list of 10-20 people that you know. Ask each of them for an investment of $10,000 for a 7% stake in your company. If 10 of them agree, you will have $100,000, and you only gave out 70% of your business. The remaining 30% is still yours for FREE.

You just have to be creative, remember when there is a strong will power to achieve something, there is always a way to get there.

COMMERCIAL LENDERS

Banks are very unlikely to invest in startup businesses. However, they can be a source of financing for stable, established small businesses. Under federal law, banks are not allowed to invest in businesses in general, but if you are one individual who wants to borrow money from a bank, that turns into a very valid possibility.

If you have enough assets to serve as collateral and there is enough stability predicted for your personalized, small-scale endeavor, a bank may loan you money.

SMALL BUSINESS ADMINISTRATION (SBA) LOANS

The SBA offers loans to both startups and small businesses. These loans are often administered by local banks and typically require the business owner to provide at least one-third of the required capital. The rest of the loan amount must also be backed by personal assets.

In my experience, I have noticed typically smaller local banks are more inclined to offer loans to local family-owned bakeries, restaurants, coffee shops, and another similar type of businesses than some of the bigger banks.

But that may not be true for every part of the country, so it is best to talk to at least 3-4 banks and try to get the feel if they are really into these sort of business financing or not before you submit your application.

Sometimes your local business brokers or commercial real estate agents can guide you to the right bank as they often deal with similar situations and knows which banks are more favorable to these sort of loans. You can also ask your bank that you deal with every day and ask for their advice.

Now once you narrow down to say two banks, visit them, have a meeting with their loan officer and see what their requirements are.

Just remember every bank will have similar requirements, but still, they can vary widely based on many factors like how much down payment they require, how much collateral they will need from you to even if they offer some SBA assisted loans or not.

Your goal would be to deal with a bank that offers SBA loan, SBA stands for Small Business Administration. This is where federal government guarantees part of your loan to the bank.

Most times SBA offers some sort of guarantee(typically 50-80%) on your behalf to the bank, so banks are somewhat more lenient in approving the loan as they are not in the risk for the total amount they are giving you. But the downside to this is the amount of paperwork you have to furnish is monumental in most cases.

SBA's requirements can be broad and extensive, so be prepared to gather up a lot of paperwork.

Another drawback to SBA loan is it can take up to 4 months to get approval from them as they run slower than most banks and in their defense, they do have a lot of applicants that are submitting applications. Which they have to go through all them, it is always first come first serve, so be patient.

But if you have larger down payment (30% or higher) or have some good collateral to offer, then you can opt out on SBA loans and get most any banks to provide you a conventional business loan. Provided you have all your ducks in a row like your credit is in excellent shape, your tax returns show good incomes for previous years and so on so forth.

When you talk to any banks, they will hand you something call a loan package, most times the package will have a checklist of documents that you need to furnish to them along with a loan application and some other waiver forms depending on your bank.

One thing to keep in mind, all banks and commercial lenders do have to follow certain guideline that is set by federal and state banking authorities. Also, every bank will look at something call LTV (Loan to Value) ratio of the property or business you are looking to buy.

LTV is essentially where banks look at the actual value of the business you are looking to buy or lease and how much of that value they can loan you.

Let's look at the list of documents you will need to get ready to submit to your bank. Some of these items I will mention here may not be on your bank's checklist but do gather them anyway as it will make you look more professional and business-like.

LIST OF DOCUMENTS YOU WILL NEED FOR YOUR LOAN APPLICATION

1. You need to get copies of at least last three years of personal tax returns, make sure the copies are signed.

2. Your resume (they may not even ask you for it, but remember the person that may approve your loan may never meet you but this way at least he or she gets to see who you are and how qualified you are it always helps)

3. Copy of your Corp. Articles, (yes you have to get this done before you even apply for your loan, I will touch on how to file a corporation in the next chapter)

4. Personal financial statement for all Corp. Officers or members, make sure to sign it, if you are married and file joint tax returns than your wife needs to have one prepared for her as well or you can make a joint personal financial statement for both of you and make sure to both sign that document.

5. Copy of the commercial appraisal (in the event you are buying a location instead of leasing)

6. Copy of signed purchase agreement and Letter of intent (in the event you are buying)

7. Copy of your EIN (Employer's Identification Number) issued by the IRS

8. Copy of all member/partner's Driver's licenses and social security cards

9. A well thought out and expertly written Business Plan (not a store bought one or copy-pasted one, one that is written for your specific business, get help if you need to,

but this has to be a well thought out plan, do it like your life depends on it trust me on this.)

10. Last but the least the loan application all filled out, use a computer and printer if possible, if not write very clearly, so it is easy to read.

11. A cover letter addressed to the loan department where you describe what is in the package and thanking them for reviewing your loan application and lastly tell them where they easily reach you if they need further help or other documents from you, it just makes you look more professional.

Now, remember to organize these papers with nice tabs and in a binding folder where anyone can open the folder, looking at the tabs, they can go directly to that specific section.

If you are applying for an SBA specific business loan then SBA may also give you a loan package with some more documents and forms to fill out, but they will mostly ask for the same as I just mentioned.

But yes they will have you fill out many more forms, and don't worry you do not have to visit SBA office separately they work through your local banks so the loan officer you deal with will furnish you all of that

You must read the fine print involved in each of these funding options, as their regulations will change depending on the company you interact with. What best worked for me were angel investors. That path diminished the pressure of needing to have a concrete established business for an idea I knew would work; it would just take a bit more time.

Sometimes it may help to contact a trusted friend or family member with a larger income who is willing to back you for either angel investors or the other funding options, so there is more good faith established between you and the loaners.

After you have funding in place and you are getting ready to file your paperwork in order to start your business, it is important that you determine a business structure that meets your needs.

Starting a business is fun, but a little overwhelming and certainly confusing if you are unsure as to what to do next. By this point, you have both a business and a financial plan, as well as a solid idea of where to get your funding from. So, what now?

One of the more confusing areas is choosing a business structure. Even if you know the options, how can you know which is right for your business? In this chapter we are going to look at the types of business structures and how you can choose the right one for your preferences.

Sole Proprietorship

This is one of the most common structures for small businesses. The business is entirely yours, and you will assume complete responsibility. This means you get all the profits but are also liable for all losses.

Who Should Choose It

When you choose to run your small business by yourself, you are going to be in charge of all the aspects involved in running the business.

If this is appealing to you, then a sole proprietorship may be a good option, so long as you understand the responsibilities involved and have a Plan B in case the business did not turn out the way you intended it to at first or may need modifications.

How to Form

This is one of the easiest business structures to form. In fact, there is no action required on your part to form this business structure. You will need to do some work for licensing and regulations depending on the industry your business is in, so you'll want to check with the local secretary of state about the necessary regulations.

In addition, if you are going to do business under a name that isn't your own, you'll need to file a DBA or Doing Business As.

WHAT YOU NEED TO KNOW

While a sole proprietorship is basic and fairly simple, there are some things to consider:

1. A sole proprietorship is also known as a "pass-through" tax entity. This means that all profits and losses are passed through you as the business owner and you need to report them on your taxes. So, you'll need to file a Schedule C, Form 1040, and Schedule SE when filing your taxes.

2. While you can be the sole owner under a sole proprietorship, this doesn't mean you can't have employees. However, having employees will make your taxes slightly more complicated.

3. It can be more difficult to raise money with a sole proprietorship as well. This is because you won't be able to sell stock in your company and thus won't be able to increase your company's wealth as quickly as other types of business structures.

4. Getting a bank loan as a sole proprietorship is also more problematic since you are less credible from the banks' point of view unless you have a solid financial backer.

5. Lastly, be aware that you are assuming full responsibility. If you can't pay your debts or if your business fails, then your personal assets are at risk. You will also be held liable if there are any legal issues, so the authorities can go after those personal assets and use them to pay off any investors.

PARTNERSHIP

When you choose to partner with someone for your business you may choose to share ownership, so all parties involved have a share over input and participation in the company, this is still a simple business structure.

Who Should Choose It

This is a slightly bigger version of a sole proprietorship. It is best for when two or more people want to form an agreement and start a business together. The parties will be equal participants and bring their own unique viewpoints to the business.

How to Form

As with a sole proprietorship, doing business with someone basically forms the basis of a partnership. If you plan to do business other than your name or that of your partner, then you need to file a DBA.

Certain licenses or permits are also needed depending on your type of business and the state you operate in, so check with your local secretary of state office for specifics.

What You Need to Know

It is important to note that there are different types of partnership options. The type you choose will depend on how long you want to be partners and what active role each party is taking in the business.

General Partnership.

Assumes all parties involved are involved equally: including all profits, liabilities, and duties. If anything is intentionally unequally split, then it needs to be noted in the official partnership agreement.

Limited Partnership.

This format is often used when one partner serves in an investor role with limited input into the operations of the company. This format is more complex and typically isn't used as often unless the intention is to eventually become a sole proprietor.

Joint Venture.

If you are planning to partner with someone for just one specific project, then the joint venture format is best. It is similar to a general partnership but is only for a specific period of time to complete a single project.

Before choosing a partnership, there are three things you need to consider, of course:

1. While not necessary, it is highly recommended that you outline a partnership agreement before starting a partnership. This will help ensure you start the

business on the right foot and establish the limitations for both parties. It will allow you to clearly define what each person is responsible for and what will happen should you decide to quit working together.

2. Like a sole proprietorship, partnerships are also "pass-through" tax entities. This means all profits and losses are passed to the partner owners, so the risk and benefit factors are still the same, which is something both people involved need to take in mind at all times.

3. Since you should have a lawyer review your partnership agreement, you'll want to take this added cost into account when calculating your startup costs.

Limited Liability Corporation (LLC)

With the two previous options, the scariest factor is that you'll be personally responsible if something goes wrong with the business and you or your partner may not be able to pay for the resulting costs.

The LLC structure offers you the best of everything. It gives you the flexibility of the previous two structures, but limits the responsibilities of those involved, like a corporate structure.

WHO SHOULD CHOOSE IT

If you have assets that you want to protect without involving your business, an LLC is your best choice. It can also be a good option if you own a business within an industry that is prone to lawsuits so you can protect your personal assets.

HOW TO FORM

Forming an LLC is a little more difficult since you'll have to choose a compliant name, file articles of organization, and create an operating agreement. You'll also need to file for specific licenses or permits and a DBA if you need one.

WHAT YOU NEED TO KNOW

While choosing an LLC has many advantages, it is a more complex structure, and you'll need to consider the following to determine if an LLC structure is right for you.

1. An LLC is considered a pass-through tax entity, like the two previous structures. However, under an LLC structure, you are only taxed on your share of the profits, which are filed under your personal taxes.

2. In almost all states except Massachusetts, you can form an LLC with a single individual. In some situations, starting an LLC can be a better option than starting a sole proprietorship.

CORPORATION

This is likely the structure most think of when it comes to business. A corporation involves shareholders, a complex legal structure, and intricate tax requirements.

WHO SHOULD CHOOSE IT

This is one of the most complicated business structures to handle, so you may not want to choose it if you are running the business yourself or just partnering with a few people unless you have prior experience in the field.

A corporation is often recommended for companies that are larger, more established, have many employees, intend to sell stock, scale quickly, have outside investors, or any combination of these.

How to Form

The first step in forming a corporation is to register your business name. You'll also need to file articles of incorporation and get a Federal Tax Identification number or EIN for that business as a separate entity.

What You Need to Know

It is important to know there are several types of corporate structures to choose from. The most common type is known as a C Corporation, or C Corp. There are also a few others you should know about before choosing this option. Let's look at all of them.

C Corporation

The most common type of corporation. All shareholders combine the funds and are then given stock in the business. From the standpoint of the IRS, a C Corp is a completely separate tax entity so that the company can take tax deductions.

Not to mention, profits are taxed twice; from the business standpoint and your personal taxes if you get income in the form of dividends. However, you can minimize this taxation with a good tax planning strategy.

S Corporation

The main difference between this structure and a C Corp is that profits and losses can be passed through to your personal tax return. In order to form an S Corp, you need to set up your business as a corporation first, then request S Corp status. It is best to speak with an attorney before starting this process, just to ensure you are well-informed on the benefits and risks involved.

B Corporation

If your business has a social mission or a good cause as its foundation, then you may want to consider this option. It is basically a C Corp that has been vetted and approved for B Corp status. Some states give this form of the corporation a tax break.

While a corporation as a whole offers key advantages, it isn't the best option for everyone. There are a few things to keep in mind before choosing this option:

1. Since a corporation is its own entity, your personal assets are fully protected, so if worst comes to worst, you will not need to lose your personal assets such as a previously established business or a house.

2. A corporation has a greater chance of raising capital. All corporations can sell stock which will increase their ability to attract investors.

3. Since a corporation files taxes separately from personal taxes, your business will be eligible for additional tax breaks.

4. The biggest downside to a corporation is the fact that it is the most complicated structure. So be prepared to do a lot of work (typically involving a lawyer's assistance) to establish a solid corporation.

Depending on what your current income is, and how large you want your business to become, the structure or type of corporation you choose is bound to help you reach the next level in your endeavors. I personally suggest picking one with a realistic mindset.

So, not overestimating where you want your business to go, but also without blind fear on the matter. Consulting with established business owners helps a great deal, as I discovered on my journey. Through this method, you find out the more intricate between-the-lines contexts of each structure and corporation, as well as the benefits and risks for each.

Once you have decided on a business structure, another important thing you want to consider and get set up is insurance. Let's look at everything you need to know and consider when it comes to business insurance.

BUSINESS INSURANCE

When you start a business, the last thing you want to do is spend money for protection you don't need. However, ignoring important insurance can also have a major impact on your ability to function as a business and make a decent profit.

So, what level of insurance is adequate for your business? The truth is there is no straight answer other than it is most likely more than you are expecting.

While a business owner's general policy will fit most general needs, it may not cover everything. Let's look at the types of insurance policies available to business owners and whether or not you need any of them.

GENERAL LIABILITY INSURANCE OR COMMERCIAL LIABILITY

What It Covers

It protects from a wide range of lawsuits that come from negligence while covering the cost of defense, claims for bodily harm or property damage, personal injury, and advertising damages related to libel or slander.

Required

Oftentimes this insurance is required for a physical business to be able to rent space or secure a loan.

Cost

Cost increases depending on exposure risk.

PRODUCT LIABILITY INSURANCE

What It Covers

If your business makes, distributes, or sells a product then you are exposed to product liability since nearly all products have the potential to cause personal or property damage. This type of insurance will help protect your company from negligence, breach of warranty, product defects, and faulty instructions. It can also help cover you against the cost of recalls.

Required

While not required, it is often included in a business owner's policy. If you are providing parts or services to a larger company, you may be required to maintain this insurance as a part of your contract with them, so you do not become an added cost for them in case something goes awry.

Cost

The type of product you are manufacturing will determine the cost, as the risk factor is not the same for distributing a book as it is an electrical device.

PROPERTY INSURANCE

What It Covers

This insurance protects you against damage to your workspace. This can include any type of property damage events such as fires, floods, robberies, or leaks.

Required

This insurance is required if your business is going to occupy any type of physical space.

Cost

The cost can be affected by location and environmental risk factors.

SPRINKLER LEAKAGE INSURANCE

What It Covers

Sprinkler leakage is often included in property insurance, but you should ask if it is still available if you intend to take a closer look at it. This type of insurance is important for businesses that have important documents since recreating documents can be costly and sometimes impossible depending on the water damage on your computer equipment or your file cabinets.

Required

Typically not required, but rather suggested.

Cost

Premiums can increase depending on the cost to replace documents or equipment.

PROFESSIONAL LIABILITY INSURANCE OR 'ERRORS AND OMISSIONS' OR MALPRACTICE INSURANCE

What It Covers

Nearly all businesses providing services to the public should consider the risk that people may litigate for perceived or real damages. In order to not get too deep in a legal matter, it is suggested this is covered somewhere.

Required

Not typically a requirement, although some professional boards or associations will require it for members as an extra protection measure.

Cost

The price can vary greatly depending on your profession and the specific tort law in the state.

UMBRELLA INSURANCE

What It Covers

It is basically insurance that covers you beyond the dollar limits of a general policy.

Required

Not at all, but still relevant in its own way, depending on what it pertains to.

Cost

Often cheap since claims that reach the level of umbrella insurance are rare.

WORKER'S COMPENSATION INSURANCE

What It Covers

This type of insurance provides compensation and medical care to employees injured on the job. The employee often gets compensation in exchange for giving up the right to sue the employer.

Required

If you have employers at your care, then the answer is a solid yes. Individual states have rules on workers' compensation, so you'll need to determine the level of coverage required in your state.

Cost

The cost will be influenced by the state laws and programs. It can also be influenced by the type of business you have and whether or not it is likely to have more claims. In addition, if your company has a history of making claims then your premiums will be higher.

INTERNET BUSINESS INSURANCE

What It Covers

This insurance is important for the small to medium-sized companies that do business online. It helps provide you with protection against security and privacy breaches. You may want to consider this policy even if you are a more offline business with multiple locations that digitally transmit information.

Required

No, as it is more of a factor that depends on what type of business you have and it is more on the low-risk than anything else.

Cost

This is a new type of insurance, and the cost often is determined by online activity and the type of information that needs to be protected, such as debit or credit cards, bank transactions, addresses, passwords, and other valuable customer and personal information.

CRIME AND FIDELITY INSURANCE

What It Covers

This insurance helps protect you from workplace fraud and theft.

Required

Not typically, but may be required by a few business types.

Cost

You can reduce cost with strong policies and audit controls along with performing background checks on employees.

BUSINESS INTERRUPTION EXPENSE INSURANCE

What It Covers

If your business should become disabled for any reason, this policy will cover financial outlays and reimburse any lost profits until the business can resume.

Required

No, but strongly recommended.

Cost

If you get this policy, you should make sure it has extra expense coverage. This can help you to rent an alternative location and resources while everything is getting sorted out in your original location.

BUSINESS AUTO INSURANCE

What It Covers

If your employees spend a lot of time on the road in their own vehicles or company vehicles, then this insurance is very important.

Required

If your business owns or requires any kind of vehicle, this insurance is mandatory and is also known as fleet insurance.

Cost

The price of auto insurance varies by state.

Insurances are often seen as something only more paranoid individuals attain for matters that could be easily prevented with proper equipment.

For example, a water damage insurance is not necessary for a business located in a location where floods are improbable, and important files are placed in waterproof containers at a higher floor level, and online documents are constantly backed in USB drives or other methods.

However, if you have employers under your care, then it is imperative you get them insurance in order to give them a better work environment. These are preventative measures you must take regardless of what type of insurance you are considering. Now, the type you go for depends on the business you intend to start.

Now that we know about the insurance aspect of starting a business, we should move on to looking at the legal paperwork you need to complete.

BUSINESS LEGAL PREPARATION

TAX AND BUSINESS FORMS

The only businesses that don't file annual income tax returns are partnerships since they file an information return. The form you file will depend on how you've organized your business, in other words.

Businesses typically pay taxes quarterly to both federal and state governments. Let's look at some of the common federal business and tax forms that you need to file when starting a business.

I-9 EMPLOYMENT ELIGIBILITY VERIFICATION

Employers need to complete and retain this form for each individual they hire within the United States. This includes citizen and noncitizen employees. The employer must examine the employment eligibility and identity documents. The form must be then kept for three years from the date of hire or for one year after employment is terminated, whichever is later.

SS-4: EMPLOYER ID NUMBER (EIN) APPLICATION FORM

The EIN is also known as a Federal or Employer Tax Identification Number and is used to identify a business entity. You can apply for this in a number of ways, but most prefer online.

It is a free service offered through the Internal Revenue Service. Check with your state to determine if you need a state number or charter.

Here is a link to IRS website where you can download or fill out the form online.

https://www.irs.gov/businesses/small-businesses-self-employed/how-to-apply-for-an-ein

Form SS-4
(Rev. January 2010)
Department of the Treasury
Internal Revenue Service

Application for Employer Identification Number

(For use by employers, corporations, partnerships, trusts, estates, churches, government agencies, Indian tribal entities, certain individuals, and others.)

► See separate instructions for each line.   ► Keep a copy for your records.

OMB No. 1545-0003

EIN

Type or print clearly.

1 Legal name of entity (or individual) for whom the EIN is being requested

2 Trade name of business (if different from name on line 1)

3 Executor, administrator, trustee, "care of" name

4a Mailing address (room, apt., suite no. and street, or P.O. box)

5a Street address (if different) (Do not enter a P.O. box.)

4b City, state, and ZIP code (if foreign, see instructions)

5b City, state, and ZIP code (if foreign, see instructions)

6 County and state where principal business is located

7a Name of responsible party

7b SSN, ITIN, or EIN

8a Is this application for a limited liability company (LLC) (or a foreign equivalent)?   ☐ Yes ☐ No

8b If 8a is "Yes," enter the number of LLC members ►

8c If 8a is "Yes," was the LLC organized in the United States?   ☐ Yes ☐ No

9a Type of entity (check only one box). Caution. If 8a is "Yes," see the instructions for the correct box to check.
- ☐ Sole proprietor (SSN) _____
- ☐ Partnership
- ☐ Corporation (enter form number to be filed) ►
- ☐ Personal service corporation
- ☐ Church or church-controlled organization
- ☐ Other nonprofit organization (specify) ►
- ☐ Other (specify) ►
- ☐ Estate (SSN of decedent) _____
- ☐ Plan administrator (TIN) _____
- ☐ Trust (TIN of grantor)
- ☐ National Guard   ☐ State/local government
- ☐ Farmers' cooperative   ☐ Federal government/military
- ☐ REMIC   ☐ Indian tribal governments/enterprises

Group Exemption Number (GEN) if any ►

9b If a corporation, name the state or foreign country (if applicable) where incorporated

State

Foreign country

10 Reason for applying (check only one box)
- ☐ Started new business (specify type) ►
- ☐ Hired employees (Check the box and see line 13.)
- ☐ Compliance with IRS withholding regulations
- ☐ Other (specify) ►
- ☐ Banking purpose (specify purpose) ►
- ☐ Changed type of organization (specify new type) ►
- ☐ Purchased going business
- ☐ Created a trust (specify type) ►
- ☐ Created a pension plan (specify type) ►

11 Date business started or acquired (month, day, year). See instructions.

12 Closing month of accounting year

13 Highest number of employees expected in the next 12 months (enter -0- if none). If no employees expected, skip line 14.

Agricultural	Household	Other

14 If you expect your employment tax liability to be $1,000 or less in a full calendar year and want to file Form 944 annually instead of Forms 941 quarterly, check here. (Your employment tax liability generally will be $1,000 or less if you expect to pay $4,000 or less in total wages.) If you do not check this box, you must file Form 941 for every quarter. ☐

15 First date wages or annuities were paid (month, day, year). Note. If applicant is a withholding agent, enter date income will first be paid to nonresident alien (month, day, year).

16 Check one box that best describes the principal activity of your business.   ☐ Health care & social assistance   ☐ Wholesale-agent/broker
- ☐ Construction   ☐ Rental & leasing   ☐ Transportation & warehousing   ☐ Accommodation & food service   ☐ Wholesale-other   ☐ Retail
- ☐ Real estate   ☐ Manufacturing   ☐ Finance & insurance   ☐ Other (specify) ►

17 Indicate principal line of merchandise sold, specific construction work done, products produced, or services provided.

18 Has the applicant entity shown on line 1 ever applied for and received an EIN?   ☐ Yes ☐ No
If "Yes," write previous EIN here ►

Third Party Designee

Complete this section only if you want to authorize the named individual to receive the entity's EIN and answer questions about the completion of this form.

Designee's name

Designee's telephone number (include area code) ►

Address and ZIP code

Designee's fax number (include area code)

Under penalties of perjury, I declare that I have examined this application, and to the best of my knowledge and belief, it is true, correct, and complete.

Name and title (type or print clearly) ►

Applicant's telephone number (include area code)

Applicant's fax number (include area code)

W-2: WAGE AND TAX STATEMENT FORM

This form is used to report wages or salaries that you pay to employees within a calendar year, along with any taxes withheld from them. It also reports FICA taxes to the Social Security Administration.

A W-2 must be filled out for all employees that are receiving a salary, wage, or any other form of compensation. The W-2 must be delivered to employees no later than January 31st.

W-4: Employee's Withholding Allowance Certificate Form

This form is filled out by the employees to note deductions so you can determine how many taxes are withheld from wages or salaries. This is ideally the exact amount due on the employee's 1040 form at the end of the tax year.

1040 Schedule C or C-EZ: Profit or Loss from Business (Sole Proprietorship) Form

Anyone who is self-employed needs to use a 1040 Schedule C to report their income or losses, as well as to calculate self-employment taxes. You are able to use a 1040 Schedule C-EZ if you have profit and any of the following:

- Expenses under $5,000

- No employees

- No inventory

- Not using depreciation or deducting the cost of your home

1099 MISC: Miscellaneous Income Form

This form is used to report miscellaneous income such as fees, rents, commissions, royalties, prizes, awards, or income earned as a non-employee.

Opening a Commercial Bank Account

This is one important step, but it can only be done after you have a fully executed article of incorporation which has been approved by the state, and you have an EIN number assigned by the IRS.

Once you have these two documents, you should be able to go to a bank and open your first commercial bank account.

But remember to check and understand various types of commercial checking account fees, you want to find a bank that offers free or almost free commercial checking account because some larger banks can charge you hundreds of dollars each month depending on how many transactions you do. Make sure to ask and shop around before you sign on the dotted line.

FOOD PERMIT

If you are opening a food-related retail business, one of the most essential steps in your licensing process should be to discuss your proposed plan and operation with your local city and county health department. As they will be the ultimate authority to issue you a food permit without which you can operate your business.

Next step would be to go to your local city and county business licensing office and find out what type of business and regulatory licenses you are required to have. It should take a few days to get your licenses and permits in place, and then you are finally and officially in business.

You also need to attend a 4-6 hour class to obtain your SafeServ permit. This is a certificate that ensures that the manager or the owner of any food-related businesses know how to handle food safely.

Each establishment needs to have minimum one person who is certified in the SafeServ program

Here is the link to Safe Serve site so you can find out more about how to attend their class and get certified.

https://www.servsafe.com/

COPYRIGHT, TRADEMARK, AND PATENTS

When it comes to starting a business, not many give thought to protecting their intellectual property. In fact, you should protect it the same as you would any other asset. In order to do this, you first need to understand intellectual property rights and why it is so important to claim your ideas and your creations as your own.

There are two common forms of intellectual property protections that you'll likely be faced with when owning a business: copyright and trademark. These two are often confused, but they both protect different types of intellectual property.

Once you know the differences, you'll be able to understand how you can use both to protect the creative output of your business and secure your assets properly.

COPYRIGHT

Copyright is defined by the Library of Congress as "a form of protection grounded in the U.S. Constitution and granted by law for original works of authorship fixed in a tangible medium of expression." So, loosely translated, what does this mean exactly and how does it work for your business?

Copyright works for any creative products that are written on paper, in design, or anywhere else. Copyright exists from the moment your work is created, whether you have it registered through the Copyright Office or not.

However, registering is a good idea if you want it to hold up in a court of law. If you copyright your work, then you retain the right to sue for infringement.

REGISTERING YOUR COPYRIGHT

Once you have obtained copyright, you will be able to protect works that include literature, drama, music, poetry, movies, songs, software, and architecture. To register them, you'll have to submit an application to the U.S. Copyright Office and pay a fee; all of this can be done online.

In addition to the ability to sue for copyright infringement, you are also granted prima facie status in court if you register your copyright within five years of the work's publication. This means that the copyright is accepted as fact and cannot be argued with in any manner.

Copyright protection also extends beyond the U.S. to many other nations. The protections expire after the life of the creator plus 70, 95, or 120 years depending on the type of work being protected.

TRADEMARK

The U.S. Patent and Trademark Office (USPTO) defines a trademark as "a word, phrase, symbol and/or design that identifies and distinguishes the source of the goods of one party from those of others."

When you obtain federal trademark protection, you can use the trademark nationwide and have the ability to sue in federal court. This can triple the damages of infringement and nationwide injunctions in order to prevent the use of your trademark.

OBTAINING A TRADEMARK

Similar to the copyright, registering your trademark is entirely voluntary. You can affix a ™ superscript after your brand or product to adopt what is known as "common law" rights. Once registered with the USPTO, you can affix a ® superscript to denote legal ownership.

To register your trademark, you need to undergo an application process and pay a filing fee of $225. Trademarks never expire once they are registered, so it is a small prie to pay for the safety of your creativity and profit.

PATENT

A patent is defined by the USPTO as, "a limited duration property right relating to an invention... in exchange for public disclosure of that invention." A patent can include a machine, manufactured goods, industrial processes, or chemical compositions.

When a patent is in effect, the holder has the right to exclude others from making, using, or selling the invention without their explicit legal permission. The patent holder has the responsibility for enforcing the patent by taking the responsible party to court if there are any infringements. The U.S. federal government doesn't enforce patents, so it is entirely up to you to make your voice heard.

OBTAINING A PATENT

There are several types of patents that you can apply for, so the first thing you need to do is determine which patent is best for your invention. The USPTO website features an application process for patents, for example.

In addition, you'll have to pay a filing fee of $130 to $3,000 depending on what patent you are applying for. Design patents expire 15 years after they are issues, while utility and plant patents expire 20 years from the filing date.

When you are starting a business, you need to consider building a brand. Whether it is your business name, logo, color palette, website, or marketing method, all good businesses need an excellent brand in order to attract potential customers.

It isn't that difficult to build a brand, as it can be done with the three Cs: clarity, consistency, and constancy. This means you need to build a clear story and send that story out to your target audience so they will identify you among your competitors. Let's look at the basics of building a brand and promoting it to help you in the final step to starting your business.

Choosing a Business Name

While choosing a business name may seem like a minor detail, it is just as important as the rest of the steps we've discussed within this book. You need to give a lot of thought and attention to choosing the perfect business name.

Consumers make a lot of assumptions based on your business name, so you want to choose one that represents what you want your business to be and something that you plan to maintain for years to come.

The Importance of a Name

Many consumers will judge a business solely by their name. You can name your business after a product you make or service you offer, but you need to consider what may happen if you eventually stop making that product or expand to include other services.

Making a Choice

Choosing the right name saves you both time and money. You don't have to spend as much on advertising and marketing when your business name already conveys the right message. A good name will also elevate you above the competition and help your business grow. Deciding on a great name starts with defining your business, the brand, and the goals.

The name you pick should be one that expresses how your business operates. To achieve this, you need to avoid literal descriptions of your product or service. If you invent a new type of corkscrew, you probably should not name it something like 'New Corkscrew,' or if you want to sell soap you do not just come up with, 'Soap Store.' You should also avoid geographic references that make limit the scope of your marketplace unless that is the intention.

On the other hand, you want to avoid choosing a name that tries to say everything about your business, so the mystery is kept alive.

There are a lot of trade-offs that goes into designing a business name. If you choose one that is too unique or cryptic, you'll be spending a lot of marketing time, effort, and money explaining the meaning of the name rather than drawing in potential customers.

Invented names can also have a negative impact in other languages or cultures, as the word of your choice can mean something entirely different in another tongue.

Once you have developed a strong name that covers all of these characteristics and is generally understood by your target audience, you can focus on building your brand and marketing campaign.

LOGO DESIGN

A major part of building up your brand is designing your identity. This includes a logo, imagery, color palettes, and other things to reinforce your brand story. Remember to be consistent throughout the visual aspect of your business.

Do not start out with a purple lettering logo unless you intend to keep that purple lettering for the next couple of years before a grand reopening or something around that neighborhood.

There are a few great online talent hiring sites that can help you design your brand at a very reasonable cost.

- 99designs.com
- Upwork.com
- Freelancer.com
- Fiverr.com

If you have limited budget try fiverr.com. This is a place where you can find talents from all around the world ready to take any task for $5 only. This is my go to site for many jobs like simple logo designs to social media marketing.

Once you have your logo, make sure to order business cards, bags, boxes and other packaging accessories for your business. You can get a local printing press to do this job or find many online printing services that can do the same job for much cheaper.

INTERNET PRESENCE

Another important part of developing your brand is to have a website that looks fantastic while also being easy to navigate. Essentially, you want to create a website that has the best of both form and function; it should reflect the logo and imagery of your business while reinforcing the color palette and brand story.

If you have a website that is very pretty but too complex, you may lose customers just the same way if you had an easier site surrounded by red-colored Comic Sans on top of a bright blue background.

Let's avoid those types of color combinations and stick with something that is simple, clean, and easily understood. Make sure you regularly update your website to meet the expectations of your customer feedback.

SPREADING YOUR BRAND

After you've developed a strong brand identity, you need to spread it. To do so, you should use various marketing channels. Choose marketing that helps to connect with potential customers in person as well as online, so you can target the maximum number of people at one time.

This is essential to successful branding, and also where consistency is important, since regular appearances of your brand will reinforce your identity to the ideal customer base. Let's look at some marketing channels you can consider.

OUTREACH

By now you probably have a decent idea of which marketing segments to target. You need to consider your target audience and go to them, rather than waiting for them to come to you.

For a store-based business you want to gain a foothold in the community, and the best way to do this is through networking events and social situations where you are able to spread the word and give samples of your products or services as well as having business cards at the ready. Offering discounts is also another nice detail to add to any grand opening.

SEARCH ENGINE OPTIMIZATION (SEO)

SEO is the process of boosting your website's ranking on search engine results through keywords. This helps to grow something termed "organic" traffic, or potential leads that find your company while searching for a general product or service.

You can boost your rankings by creating intelligent and accurate information related to your product or service industry. This is an excellent way to boost your marketing and attract potential customers without having to pay for advertising.

SOCIAL MEDIA

Social media is a great option when it comes to putting a human face to your brand and drawing in your target audience. Consider the brand story you've been telling and develop a consistent social media voice to convey the message. Always stick to your brand story and have frequent social media engagement in order to cultivate a strong brand.

Now you are ready to get out there and start your business. In conclusion, I want to tie together all that I've told you and break down the process for two major business startups: home-based and store-based.

HOME-BASED BUSINESS NEEDS

There are several well-known businesses that started out in their owner's homes. In fact, the statistics have shown that nearly 70 percent of all U.S. businesses start at home. Before you decide to start a home-based business, there are a few questions you need to ask yourself:

- Do you have the focus and motivation to work from home?

- Do you have someone who can help if your business gets stalled?

- How will you determine if your business is successful?

- How do you plan to handle the administrative portion of the business?

- Do you have what it takes to run a home based business?

- Do you have the space you need as well as the right type of environment in your home to regularly deliver your products or services to customers?

It is important that you also consider the benefits of a home-based business. This will help you determine if starting a home-based business is the best option for you.

- Financial Savings

- Tax Incentives

- Flexible Scheduling

- Convenience

- Working on Your Passion

- Greater Accomplishment

However, you also want to be aware of the disadvantages. All home-based businesses come with some disadvantages.

- Isolation from Others

- More Effort

- Less Oversight

- Difficult to Find Customers

- Appears Unprofessional

If you are certain that starting a home-based business is the best route for you, then consider the following checklist to help you get your home-based business started.

- ☐ Write a Business Plan

- ☐ Set up a Work Station

- ☐ Legally Establish Your Business

- ☐ Establish Your Tax Needs

- ☐ Register Your Business Name

- ☐ Obtain Necessary Insurance

There are also a few things you need to do to have a successful business, such as:

- Keep financial accounts separate.

- Set and keep specific business hours.

- Market your business.

- Network with other business owners.

- Spend as little as possible.

I personally have a home-based business after setting up a work station in an extra room my spouse, and I typically saved for guests but otherwise would rarely use.

It needed a few changes, such as other kinds of furniture and a more reliable air conditioner, but for the most part, it became a solid place where I could keep my files organized while creating my product in peace.

From time to time I do need to rent a small studio for the larger, more complex designs I work on, of course, at a small price.

Now, if starting a home-based business doesn't sound right for you, consider opting for a standard store-based business instead. Let's look at what you'll need.

BRICK & MORTAR BUSINESS NEEDS

No matter whether you choose to start a home-based business or a store-based business, the process is never too easy. However, there are a few extra steps involved in setting up a store-based business. Specifically, there are ten things you need to address first:

1. Create a mission statement.

2. Clearly present your business.

3. Clearly define your finances.

4. Create a plan for customer service.

5. Investigate your retail space.

6. Choose a retail location with great customer traffic.

7. Create a well-defined store layout.

8. Legally establish your business.

9. Finalize the products you're offering.

10. Network with your potential customers.

Perhaps you are somewhere between these two; you don't want to start a home-based business, and the idea of starting a retail business seems like too much trouble. If this is the case, there are some alternative options.

ALTERNATIVE BUSINESS STARTUP IDEAS TO EXPLORE

When you are starting a business, you want to make sure you choose a platform that is not only successful for your business, but also for you. If you start a business that you can't properly maintain in a workspace you are uncomfortable and disorganized in, you will inevitably fail.

So, choose a business platform that you can do well with. If a home-based business or a retail store isn't right for you, consider some of the following out-of-the-box ideas for a startup business.

KIOSKS

This option gives you a retail store in a small and manageable space within a high traffic area. The concept works if you are only going to have a small amount of inventory or seasonal retail. Kiosks are often thought of as malls, but they can also be found at transportation hubs and event venues.

There are many advantages to starting a kiosk, especially for those new to owning a business. Kiosks have an all-in lease, meaning that all extra charges are included in your minimum rent.

The smaller area means you have cheaper rent and less overhead costs to help reduce your operational expenses. Most kiosks have an upfront cost of $2,000 to $10,000 and often don't require a long-term contract.

FARMERS MARKETS, FAIRS, AND FESTIVALS

Nearly all states have an organized farmers market, craft fair, or festival where vendors are allowed to set up a table and sell goods to those who attend. These events are most popular in spring and summer, but can sometimes be held year-round depending on where you live. Christmas bazaars, Halloween corn maze fairs, it is all fair game with the proper permission.

This makes them excellent for a side retail business. The booth fee will vary by the event, but you'll probably be paying weekly or seasonal fees. You'll also have to keep in mind the cost of licenses and permits, marketing, and setup.

To keep your business going outside of these events, you may need to develop an online presence and advertise it at your booth.

FOOD TRUCKS

Starting a restaurant is one of the most costly and riskiest business ventures you can start. With the necessity to have at least two years' worth of expenses already safe in a bank, what sounds good on paper is a pain to achieve in reality without the proper assistance. A popular alternative is the food truck.

You don't have the cost of renting a building or space, plus you don't have to worry about staffing a full kitchen and dining room. You can often rent or purchase a food truck for $40,000 to $130,000 depending on the equipment you want in it.

Statistics have also shown that food trucks have a better chance of success than a traditional restaurant.

MOBILE RETAIL UNITS

Food trucks aren't the only businesses that can be done on the go. A traveling retail store is an excellent alternative to the retail store. You can move around to different locations and keep customers updated through social media.

Mobile units can be customized and maintained far cheaper than a retail space. You can also keep moving around to profitable areas when business is slow in the last place you go to. It also provides excellent business flexibility.

Depending on the size and features of your business, you can expect the cost to be between $10,000 to $50,000.

Now I want to give you a few essential tips on balancing a business startup with a regular job.

BALANCING YOUR STARTUP WITH A FULL-TIME JOB

By now you are ready to start your business. However, not everyone is in a position to drop everything and focus solely on their new business venture. If you need to work a day job while starting your new business, it can require a bit of a balancing act.

To get through this difficult time in the process and stay on track to starting your business goals, let's look at some tips to help you.

TIME COMMITMENT

If you are going to start a new business while working a full-time job, the biggest issue is going to be finding the time. Therefore, it is important to have a schedule and stick to it; create a schedule in advance to choose days and times that you'll dedicate to your new business venture, and make sure you don't get distracted by other activities.

GRADUALLY REDUCE WORK HOURS

As your schedule and finances allow, consider reducing your time at your day job. Use the time off to focus entirely on your business venture. This may not be for everyone, but can be a great compromise without having to feel overworked.

HAVE A REALISTIC VIEW OF SACRIFICES

Starting a business is going to require sacrifices, but you need to acknowledge these in order to make matters a bit easier. Don't become discouraged by the fact that all your time is going to your new business venture and you don't see overnight results.

PAY OFF DEBTS AND CREATE AN EMERGENCY FUND

Use the fact that you are working a day job to your advantage. Use the steady income from your day job to pay off any ongoing debts that need to be taken care of immediately, and set aside some money into a savings account.

It can be a lot easier to let go of your day job and start your business when you know you have an emergency fund to get you or your family by if the new business venture doesn't take off right away.

DISCUSS THE LEGAL ASPECT

When starting a business, there are going to be a lot of legal issues. Some companies are particular about your behavior, even with what you do outside of your day job. So make sure your new business venture isn't going to affect the reputation of your current job.

If you are in doubt, go to a lawyer in order to make sure everything is in order, and you won't be causing unnecessary conflict for yourself.

SET A FINANCIAL GOAL

Establish a financial goal early on and use it as the turning point when you place all your focus on your new business. This can be a specific amount saved up from your day job or an amount you've earned from your new business venture. With a clear goal in mind, you can have a dedicated point to quit your day job.

MANAGE FREE TIME AND AVOID DISTRACTIONS

While you don't want to spend every waking hour focused on work, you still need to dedicate a lot of time to start your new business. It is going to require excellent time management and minimizing distractions. When you do these two things, you would be surprised what you can get done in a day.

That means no playing Candy Crush or Farmville instead of completing the documents you need for your business. Remember the only way to tell if your business evolves from an idea to an actual accomplishment depends on the amount of time, effort, work, and patience you are willing to put into it.

Never expect immediate results unless you have an exact plan of how you will achieve them. Faster results equal more direct involvement.

PLAN FOR FATIGUE

The reality of the situation is that it is going to be difficult maintaining two jobs at once. Stay focused and devoted, know that things are going to happen that drift slightly away from your schedule or your plan, and you just need to stay focused on the big picture. Keep in mind that once you are done, you'll have more free time with the flexible schedule of having your own business.

Give yourself a break every now and then if you are feeling blocked or particularly frustrated. On off-days, just take a deep breath and go on a walk or work on something else in order to refresh your mind and regain your confidence.

You are not Superman or Wonder Woman, so make sure you take some time instead of burning yourself out too soon and insisting on working since the quality of what you deliver will be compromised in those circumstances.

LAST WORDS

Documents, planning, lists, taxes, insurance. Boy, don't we wish we were taught this in high school. I know I got a lot more use out of reading up on how to make my own business than how to measure the area of a parallelogram, I'll tell you that. I could not have gotten to where I am without the constant support of my family and friends. Starting a business is a heavy task in almost every way.

Economically, physically, emotionally. It is something you should do only if you have complete faith in your ideas, and if you force yourself to be organized. I know that before creating my own successful business I was not the most organized person on the planet. Who knows how many times my spouse got exasperated when I forgot to add something to the grocery list or did not write down important dates on a calendar.

It wasn't until I realized I bought a notebook or two, created a new folder on my computer (backed by a USB drive), and used Excel and Word to keep track of my sales and my income that I became more responsible in the way I addressed my organizational skills.

Even though I still forget birthdays from time to time, at least I know exactly how much my business makes every week, and how to file the proper taxes for it every year.

Taking it all bit by bit in a consistent way is much more profitable in the end than trying to do it all at once, which may lead you to overlook details crucial to the success of your company. Being overwhelmed is just as problematic as procrastinating, mind you.

It is from my personal experiences that I was able to construct this guide for you, with the hopes it will allow you to save time that I lost in several hours of running around like a headless chicken looking for answers regarding

Umbrella Insurance and proper procedures for corporation forms. I hope you take my advice with a grain of salt, and back it up with acquaintances around you who have established businesses or a background in law and taxes.

I wish you the best of luck in your business venture, and I hope you find the time and financial security you have always craved. Take a chance on that big dream or big idea of yours you never thought could become more than a figment of your imagination.

It is time to make your own reality, because regardless of all the work that must be put into it, nailing your castles in the sky onto solid ground and living in them is better than just staring up at the sky and wondering what that life must be like.

Now get out there and get started with creating that next big idea.

I personally wanted to thank you for purchasing my book. As this was my first time writing, I want to ask for your forgiveness in case you find any typos or errors.

If you like my work, please leave me a review, as it would mean the world to me.

Thanks!

www.ingramcontent.com/pod-product-compliance
Lightning Source LLC
Chambersburg PA
CBHW071303220526
45468CB00001B/256